THE
POCKET
MBA

THE POCKET

MBA

A Woman's Playbook for Succeeding in Business

>>>>>>>>>>>>>>>>>>>>>>>>>>>>>>>>>>>>

JODI COTTLE

WILEY

First published in 2023 by John Wiley & Sons Australia, Ltd

Level 4, 600 Bourke St, Melbourne Victoria 3000, Australia

Typeset in WarnockPro 11/16pt

ISBN: 978-1-394-19457-5

A catalogue record for this book is available from the National Library of Australia

Cover design by Wiley

Cover image © StockSmartStart/Shutterstock,
© NadzeyaShanchuk/Shutterstock
Productivity tip icon © Scott Dunlap/iStock

Disclaimer
The material in this publication is of the nature of general comment only, and does not represent professional advice. It is not intended to provide specific guidance for particular circumstances and it should not be relied on as the basis for any decision to take action or not take action on any matter which it covers. Readers should obtain professional advice where appropriate, before making any such decision. To the maximum extent permitted by law, the author and publisher disclaim all responsibility and liability to any person, arising directly or indirectly from any person taking or not taking action based on the information in this publication. Neither the author nor the publisher are affiliated with the case study companies presented in this book, nor is any endorsement inferred based on their inclusion.

SKY3F113A56-D6B6-4CF3-A621-0D1077D8DEE7_061623

*Dedicated to women in business and leadership,
balancing the constant work, life,
and family juggle.*

CONTENTS

>>

FOREWORD

>>>>>>>>>>>>>>>>>>>>>>>>>>>>>>>>>>>

What you see is what you get with Jodi Cottle. She is self-motivated, honest, generous, focused, and she cares deeply about the people in her life, including her team members and clients.

Her genuine respect for others and strong generosity of spirit is part of the reason she has had a successful career — several times over. Since joining the Laser Clinics Australia family almost four years ago, Jodi has been an inspiring example of what can be achieved when you combine an entrepreneurial mindset with a franchise system and proven business tools that optimise productivity and foster engaged, high-performing teams.

Jodi's business is going from strength-to-strength, year-on-year. Her staff are happy, and her clients are raving fans, and none of these achievements are due to luck. They are because Jodi has dedicated her career to learning how to succeed in business. Working in different jobs, sectors, and countries, as well as for different leaders has given Jodi the opportunity to learn and test many frameworks and tools to achieve sustainable high performance — both in herself and her teams.

You might think that to be a successful business owner you have to both work on and in the business all the time. Jodi's story proves that's not the case. While Jodi is a very focussed and results-driven Laser Clinics Group franchisee, she has put in place systems and developed high-trust and empowered teams that help her have a healthy work and life balance.

And now, through this book, Jodi is sharing her 'secret sauce' to achieving success, so that other female leaders can create high-performing and sustainable workplaces — freeing them up to do more of the things they love. Jodi's story and philosophy will challenge your thinking and inspire you to try new ways of working and leading.

Jodi told me that the reason she's written this book is because she wants to create happier workplaces — where staff are engaged and empowered — by helping her fellow female leaders fix two common business problems — staff and customer turnover.

The Pocket MBA is a refreshing, easy-to-read business book that is full of smart, simple strategies and tools that can help any woman excel as a leader and business owner.

This book is an MBA-taster that gives female leaders, business owners and aspiring future franchisees unfettered access to a range of practical frameworks to take their leadership and business to the next level.

But mostly, it's a playbook for succeeding in business. Thank you Jodi, for sharing your wisdom with the next generation of business leaders and Laser Clinics Group franchisees across the globe.

Shannon Luxford
General Manager
Laser Clinics Australia

ABOUT THE AUTHOR

>>>>>>>>>>>>>>>>>>>>>>>>>>>>>>>>>>>

Born and raised in a small country town in New Zealand, Jodi spent most of her adult life in Auckland before relocating to Australia.

Jodi has been entrepreneurial from a young age, buying her first investment property at the age of 19, and building up a portfolio of six investment properties by the time she was 25. Jodi's self-taught property and investment expertise led to a career as a mortgage adviser in Auckland and, later, London. Having garnered recognition for her knowledge in the industry, she became a sought-after presenter at seminars, teaching people how to be successful in property investment.

In 2008 Jodi published *Young & Singles Guide to Property Investment*, a guide for first-time buyers that gained attention across New Zealand, where she appeared on morning TV shows and in magazines. Jodi was invited to speak regularly at industry events and became a commentator and advocate for first-time buyers.

As Jodi's career progressed, so too did her focus on business. She completed an MBA in 2013, specialising in sustainable customer experience strategies. In addition, she undertook study in applied cognitive neuroscience in the field of leadership, which quickly became a passion. Jodi applied her understanding of neuroanatomy and neurophysiology in real-world scenarios, delivering outstanding results, with a long list of stable, cohesive and high-performing teams. This high level of performance and instantly recognisable team dynamic led to career opportunities through promotion and head-hunting, as she was asked to apply her strategies to new teams, customer challenges and bigger markets.

Now living in Australia, she has established a high-performing business within the world's largest aesthetics franchise network, Laser Clinics Australia. Winning multiple awards, including Franchisee of the Year in 2021 and Clinic Manager of the Year in 2022, her business has become a well-oiled machine, using Jodi's established leadership techniques and management principles to boost team dynamics and results.

INTRODUCTION

>>

Welcome to *The Pocket MBA*! I'm so happy to have you on this journey with me. I hope that after reading this book, you'll feel the following:

1. a sense of comfort that you aren't alone in some of the issues you may have faced in your career

2. more assured in your direction and leadership ability

3. confident you finally have the tools to put in place all the stuff that enables you to kick back a little bit — without compromising your income.

Ultimately, these three things are the reasons I wrote this book! *The Pocket MBA* is all about empowering and helping you, as a woman leader, to create happier, high-performing and sustainable workplaces, freeing you up to do more of the things you love.

An express MBA ...

This book isn't a fluffy story about how I became a multimillionaire at age 40 by being a high-powered executive or a start-up genius — I am neither of those.

After working in sales roles for ten years, I moved into corporate leadership positions, building successful and high-performing teams over the next 15 years and achieving significant advancements in my career.

I have now invested in my own business as a franchisee, and my current staff turnover is less than 10 per cent — in an industry with an average turnover of 50 per cent. My business consistently sits in the top 10 nationally for its net promoter score (a customer experience metric), out of more than 200 franchises. Of all the businesses within the network of a similar age to mine, my business has over 500 per cent more five-star Google reviews.

Throughout my career, I have developed and followed certain methodologies and mindsets that helped achieve sustainable high performance — both in myself and in my teams. I provide an overview of these methods and frameworks throughout this book. Keep in mind, however, that I'm providing an *express* guide. This book is all about giving you a quick-start reference to succeeding in business as a woman leader. I provide the basics on the best methods and tools to focus on, along with some key tips and real-world anecdotes to help with your understanding. I don't provide a deep-dive into any of the particular areas — once you have a good idea about how each method can help you, your career and your business, you can research further as needed.

... For women in business

Along my journey, however, I came up against certain challenges, and many of the kinds of challenges I faced are unique to women in business. These challenges include 'mansplaining', 'hepeating', sexual harassment, discrimination and the gender pay gap.

No doubt you know all about the mansplaining phenomenon, and have likely experienced it. An interesting US study by OnePoll surveyed 2000 women in the modern workplace and found that women experience being mansplained to six times per week at work—*six* times! That's 312 times a year for a full-time employee! Now I know from personal experience how frustrating this can be but, to add insult to injury, perhaps you've also had your voice go unheard until a man repeated your words. We now also have a term for this, thanks to astronomer and physics professor Nicole Gugliucci (and her friends)—'hepeated', which Gugliucci defines as 'when a woman suggests an idea and it's ignored, but then a man says the same thing, and everyone loves it'. Thankfully, hepeating is becoming less and less accepted as more women move into leadership roles and balance up the table, but it does still exist.

Even worse for women to endure than mansplaining and hepeating is sexual harassment in the workplace—which still effects a staggering one in three women according to Safe Work Australia. What is even more alarming than that statistic is that only 17 per cent of those who experience sexual harassment make a formal complaint, with many women instead shoving it as far under the rug as it will go in an effort to forget it ever happened due to the rancid 'ick factor' it generates.

Unfortunately, many women put up with these challenges and threats day after day, feeling like they have no other choice.

Well, we do have a choice and, over time, our choices can help change the unconscious societal biases that are entrenched in our workplaces and beyond. These biases can sometimes be the crux of a woman's limiting beliefs; however, they can, and should, be overcome — and it starts with awareness, and having the right tools and methods in place.

For this reason, the first part of this book focuses on you as a female leader. I don't delve any further into how or why women face different challenges in the workplace — I'm sure you already have a pretty good awareness of the extra hurdles you've had to jump. Instead, I help you concentrate on mindset and maintaining your focus by considering your personal values, combating imposter syndrome, and controlling your environment. I also look at some brain science behind productivity and moods and how this enables you to stay in the right head space, or at least have some awareness of why you might be feeling the way you are — rather than going off on negative thought tangents.

The challenges I have faced — and the outcomes from these challenges — ultimately defined the type of leader I wanted to become. They also made me passionate about raising further awareness through my own stories, and helping provide women with the business and leadership tools they need to overcome their own challenges — whatever they may be.

My story

My early corporate career challenges of dealing with mansplaining, hepeating and, unfortunately, instances of sexual harassment often resulted in me feeling like my usual positive outlook and mindset were being repressed. Ultimately, however, these challenges made me determined to be heard.

By living through my own tale of mistreatment and coming out the other side, with the help of my next boss, I was able to identify key leadership styles that were critical to my eventual success. Later in my career, facing challenges such as the gender pay gap and being made to justify how I would balance motherhood and a career, ignited a passion to right this type of wrongdoing. So, I continued to develop my skills, which ultimately helped me build a rock-solid foundation for my business.

My experience of sexual harassment occurred early in my career, after a male boss enticed me to work for him using a big whopping salary as a carrot, as well as the autonomy and excitement of the role itself in a revolutionary start-up company. Believing it was an amazing opportunity, I accepted. However, it did not take long for the cracks to show. For example, my pay wouldn't go through, and he would use all the excuses under the sun as to why. I also started to receive weird, overly friendly texts after 5 pm that left me confused and feeling extremely uncomfortable. These included compliments on what I had been wearing that day or how I had done my hair or how sexy he found me — pass me the bucket. I found it uncomfortable to be in the same room with him towards the end and would make polite and reasonable excuses to avoid it.

I didn't let the no-pay situation go on for too long, but believing in the role and being slightly naive did mean

I stayed longer than I should have. However, when enough was enough, and the pay never amounted to what I was promised, I sued him. A few months later, I won. Unfortunately, the win felt pretty hollow — even though I was awarded what he owed me, the proceeds of the lawsuit did not cover the costs to fight it, so I was out of pocket. This landed me, at 25 years old, in considerable debt. But the principle of not letting him beat me kept me fighting till the end — debt or no debt.

Fortunately, I was plucked out of this situation by a man who was the complete opposite of my previous boss. I honestly felt at the time that he was my guardian angel, and he pretty much saved me from becoming quite anti-men in terms of bosses. I had previously worked with him in a different capacity and, when he found out about my plight, he approached me directly with a potential role. When we met up to discuss the role, my guardian angel said that he would clear my debt, justifying that he would have had to pay a similar amount as a recruitment fee if he had gone through a recruitment agent.

He further justified the payment by saying that he wanted my mind clear and not bogged down with worrying about this unfortunate financial situation. He argued he had a big job on the table, and he expected big things. He simply wanted to remove any hurdles so I could concentrate on the job. His kindness and compassion showed me what a true leader was.

Now, do you think that I worked my arse off for that man? You bet I did. And was I successful in the role, indirectly making him successful? Absolutely. To him, paying off my debt was probably just a smart business decision, but I will never forget what he did for me both materialistically and psychologically. And that was my first true experience of a 'servant leader'. Indeed, this experience started me on the journey of identifying the five leadership styles you need in order to create environments for your teams to thrive into sustainable high performance — represented in my VACAS acronym (covered in much more detail in chapter 2).

Later in my career, these earlier challenges still reared their head every now and then but, having more confidence and maturity, I was able to see them for what they were, without getting sucked into the vortex of consequential negative thought patterns. However, new challenges in this later stage of my career morphed into more tangible issues such as the gender pay gap — which in 2023 still sits at 22.8 per cent in Australia, slightly less at 17 per cent in the United States, 10 per cent for Canada and New Zealand, and 8.3 per cent in the United Kingdom. These statistics, gathered from government bodies around the world, reflect my own experience — while I knew a gender pay gap existed in New Zealand and also when I worked in the United Kingdom, I personally didn't notice it too much until I moved to Australia, where it became blindingly obvious. This makes sense, seeing the percentage gap in Australia is more than double that of New Zealand's gap.

Other challenges I faced as a woman later in my leadership career included balancing my career with relationships and/ or motherhood, and the sometimes obvious, yet conversely ambiguous, discrimination that trying to achieve this balance causes. For example, I was once going for my dream job.

I was the last one standing in the interview process and I knew it. I was the obvious choice for this role; I had the education, the industry contacts, the experience and the passion. I was down to the final stages of reference checking, which also went perfectly. All was looking good — great actually — with everything moving towards an eventual offer. Then I met the CEO.

The meeting was in an informal setting, and I was led to believe it was simply a formality due to the late stage we were at in the recruitment process. I mentioned in this meeting that I was a new mum to an eight-month-old baby. I thought we were all just building rapport and sharing about our family lives, and I didn't think anything untoward would come from it. Silly me. My being a new mum clearly raised red flags and brought into question my 'flexibility to do the role'. A short while later, I received a 'thanks but no thanks' email, with 'flexibility' stated as the culprit.

I was livid — at myself for telling the CEO I had a baby, but also at them for making this a thing that I had to now explain away. Would this have been an issue if I were a man? So, I quickly emailed back, explaining the support system I had in place — which included a nanny, a day care I happened to live opposite from, and my amazing parents who, if they needed to, would drop everything and make the trip to my city to babysit. (They did actually need to do this a number of times, by the way, with one time in particular being due to a three-week shit storm of multiple day-care contagions!) In any case, soon after I sent my reply, would you believe it, the offer came through. This also highlights an important lesson

I learned throughout my career: never accept the first 'no'. I've had to go in to bat for myself many times in my career after getting a 'no' initially. And with perseverance, I turned each pesky 'no' into a 'yes'!

Navigating these challenges later in our careers, and negotiating the constant time versus income trade-off we often make as working mothers can sometimes feel frustratingly tough and unfair. While I can't promise this book will remove these problems in society, parts II, III and IV provide inspiration to perhaps help you to overcome them personally. Additionally, the chapters in these parts help you to further your skills and confidence to build a solid foundation for your business, which will help you succeed despite whatever challenges you may face personally.

How this book is organised

Now you know a little more about me and my business and leadership journey, I invite you to settle in and enjoy this tell-it-like-it-is, no-nonsense playbook to help you develop into the best boss that you can be so you can lead yourself, your team, your customers, and your business to sustainable high performance.

I have lived and breathed the information outlined in this book through my leadership roles. Constant practice and critique have ultimately transformed these thoughts, actions and behaviours into the polished methodology it is today — and which I've included here.

This book is divided into four parts, covering leading yourself, leading your people, leading your customers and leading your business:

- *Leading yourself:* This part examines the importance of developing and understanding your own values and leadership style. It also evaluates the leadership styles that are imperative to effective leadership. I cover combatting 'imposter syndrome' and controlling your environment before it controls you, and discuss the applied cognitive neuroscience of successful leadership.

- *Leading your people:* Being a good boss pays off, and being a bad boss costs — a lot! Up to 57 per cent of employees leave jobs due to bad direct line managers, typically costing a business around 50 per cent of that employee's salary in replacement and training costs. If we take an Australian average wage of $65 000 per annum, this equates to a cost of $32 500 per year for every employee who exits. Then if we take an average small business with a team of 10 people and assume an industry average 50 per cent attrition rate, this means replacing staff is potentially costing this small business $162 500 per year. You are basically paying two and a half full-time employees who aren't even there!

  Instead, you need to know how to attract and get valuable employees to stick — and not just stick, but also contribute and be part of a stable, cohesive, and high-performing team. Creating sustainable and high-performing teams does not just happen by chance, however. This part uncovers how to find and keep people best suited to you and your business, and how to cultivate a cohesive and high-performing culture while optimising your workforce's productivity. Cognitive neuroscience themes continue in the chapters in this part.

- *Leading your customers:* Of course, another important part of running a business is knowing how to attract and get customers to stick. And, again, not just stick, but also develop into raving advocates. This part explores differentiation through aspects such as product and low-cost strategies, and examines why differentiation through customer experience is generally superior in terms of sustainability. The Sustainable Competitive Advantage (SCA) framework is introduced as the vehicle to implement your successful customer experience strategy.

- *Leading your business:* This part runs through analysing key business models and financial ratios to ensure coverage of all relevant areas when making decisions on any new business venture or market, as well as measuring your business on industry metrics.

Throughout the book, I've included bonus productivity tips. While reading through, use your device or a physical notebook nearby to keep a list of these tips, and then prioritise what is most important to you. You can then implement your chosen processes — slowly and diligently. I've also included anecdotal stories to contextualise the proven models and frameworks I cover. These models and frameworks work in the real world for real business owners and leaders. Time and time again, they have created high-performing, happy, stable and sustainable teams, along with clients who are raving advocates.

The proof is in the pudding. The information in this book has worked so well for me that my current business requires less and less of me working in it, instead allowing me to focus on the business from the comfort of home. As a result, these days I have control over my environment, and am thankful that I get to enjoy precious time with my family and everything my beautiful city has to offer, without compromising my income.

Are you ready to similarly thrive in your business? Let's begin.

PART I

>>>

LEADING YOURSELF

The chapters in this first part take up about a third of the entire book! And there is a good reason for that—these chapters are all about you. You are no good to anyone if you don't get your own direction, leadership ability, and mindset in order before trying to lead a team of people. Being a great leader isn't just about the things you organise, manage, know and impart; it's also about what you feel in your gut and being confident to follow your intuition. Most importantly, it's about how you connect with your fellow humans — whether they are your staff, colleagues, or friends and family. Women can have the upper hand in this — we are often told that we have more 'feelings' or are 'too emotional'. Well, guess what? That's great news when you're on the pathway to leadership greatness. Because those human connections and relationships you open yourself up to make the world of difference in creating a high-performing team that is sustainable.

I often notice a real lack of laughter in workplaces. One of my values is simply the word 'fun', and laughter plays a big role in that. My manager and I have giggles all the time — over all sorts of random stuff. And we often have clients comment on how much of a fun and happy workplace our clinic is. Laughter actually does a lot for the human brain to help make us think better and feel less stress — but also, it's just fun. Everything at work can sometimes be so serious and stressful and it often doesn't have to be; in fact, creating a light and jocular environment often works better. Don't worry if your staff see you having a few drinks in at a work function; that's part of them getting to know who you are. In fact, some of the tightest relationships I have with staff are built on great nights out. Women are made for developing and nurturing relationships so don't be afraid of letting people see the real you!

Relationships, of course, need to be nurtured. I don't necessarily have to go to my business every week, because my staff are all very competent. (In fact, I often find myself getting in the way when I'm there because it's a busy little clinic with many clients coming and going.) But I always go in a couple of times a week for the benefits of being face-to-face with my staff. It's so vital. I can read them like a book and intuitively pick up on things — from, for example, a simple facial expression. I'd never be able to do this if I were on the other end of a text or phone. Being able to read your people and put flames out before they truly become fires is part of the job. Again, women can have the upper hand here. We are often pretty intuitive due to how our brains have developed — so own this skill and don't be afraid to use it to your advantage!

CHAPTER 1
Leadership mindset

In this chapter, I help you work through uncovering your personal values, and show you how you can combat imposter syndrome and have greater control over your environment.

Importantly, I discuss not just how to control your environment, but also why you should in order to effectively manage your own head space sustainably. Did you know that chronic stress over a long time from a chaotic environment can actually make your brain start to shrink? This leads to all sorts of mental health issues. With all the challenges that women face in business, the best thing we can do to give us the greatest chance of success is have our own head in order, and a clear view on the direction of our lives. This chapter gets your started.

Value alignment

Do you truly know your values — that is, the beacons that guide your life? Are these values aligned with your business or workplace?

Knowing and staying true to your own values is important because they permeate many facets of your business and your actions within it. They can also help identify if you are compatible with your new or existing workplace. Values cascade to influencing your recruitment strategy and business strategy. Ultimately, they should be what your culture is built on.

When I bought into my franchised business only a month after it opened, I quickly uncovered some fundamental cultural issues that needed to be overcome. Unfortunately, the issues stemmed from the previous management. Another issue was that my staff were not having fun, so they naturally were not happy or upbeat — and in a service business, this presented a major problem. Trust was non-existent and so people did not feel secure — another major problem in the fast-paced retail environment where high productivity is needed. Having staff members who were unhappy and insecure subsequently meant focus, productivity and success were all reduced.

I had invested my life savings into this business, so I had to turn these problems around. I quickly aligned my own values to what the business needed to succeed: being upbeat, and having a sense of fun, happiness, trust, security and focus. These became what we called our 'fundamentals' — that is, our values.

Every team meeting and every strategy we undertook for approximately the next 18 months centred on reiterating these six words. Eventually, these values fully aligned with the new team I hired and the culture that followed. From there, we prospered to the point of becoming the 2021 Franchisee of the Year in Australia, and what I'm most proud of is that we are known throughout the network for our great team culture.

If you aren't already clear what your values are, the following list provides a guide to help you on your value finding mission. From the list, select three to five (maximum) attributes that you feel are most important to you. (More extensive lists of possible values are available online — see, for example, brenebrown.com/resources/dare-to-lead-list-of-values/.)

Authenticity	Faith	Individuality
Beauty	Family	Loyalty
Career	Financial Security	Peace
Compassion	Freedom	Spirituality
Education	Fun	Stability
Energy	Growth	Travel
Entrepreneurship	Health	Uniqueness

Write your chosen three to five values down somewhere you can see them every day — perhaps put them on the fridge or your bathroom mirror, for example. Let them sink into your subconscious so they become a true centre point of your life.

Whichever way you decide to uncover your own personal values, I recommend this as the first step in your leadership journey. Knowing who you are and what you value most in life allows you to remain in a more aligned, focused and productive space.

Combating imposter syndrome

Here's how authors Ruchika Tulshyan and Jodi-Ann Burey define 'imposter syndrome' (in their *Harvard Business Review* article 'Stop telling women they have imposter syndrome'):

> Imposter syndrome is loosely defined as doubting your abilities and feeling like a fraud. It disproportionately affects high-achieving people, who find it difficult to accept their accomplishments. Many question whether they're deserving of accolades.

Now consider these women:

- Sheryl Sandberg, former COO of Facebook and Meta Platforms
- Lady Gaga, singer, songwriter and pop icon
- Tina Fey, actress, comedian, writer and producer
- Jacinda Ardern, former prime minister of New Zealand.

All these amazing women have spoken publicly of suffering from imposter syndrome.

A KPMG study has found that 75 per cent of high-achieving women have reported experiencing imposter syndrome — 75 per cent! That's huge! That figure increases to 85 per cent in corporate America. Imposter syndrome is a massive problem across the globe, so if you have experienced it, you are certainly not alone.

For years I did not speak up as much as I should have in large corporate meetings, for fear of being found out as a fraud. I feared being made to feel stupid. Or watching an idea I had thoughtfully crafted in my mind and then not had the confidence to articulate slowly fade, like a dying ember in a fire. When I did muster the confidence to speak up, my idea was often 'hepeated' or talked over, so the idea went to waste again. Each time this happened, my confidence corroded a little more.

My mind did not think about the years of accolades that had earned me the right to have a seat at that table. I had earned the right to speak — and not just to speak, but also to be heard. Sometimes I felt I had earned this right more than the blokes sitting to my left and right. Why was it, then, that these male counterparts unwaveringly spoke up time and again, and were heard every time they spoke? Especially (and frustratingly) when they hepeated my ideas. My frustration at times was cry-in-the-office-toilet palpable. (In the toilet, of course, because God forbid a colleague sees us in a state of vulnerability — we have worked too hard for that, right?!) I have also often wondered why women seem to have to start at sub-zero and then work harder just to get themselves to zero — that is, a level playing field. And when we got there, we find out the field still isn't level due to the gender pay gap. Again, the frustration grows.

To make things worse, at the time imposter syndrome was coursing through my veins, I didn't know what it was — I don't think many of us did. Imposter syndrome had barely surfaced in academic literature, and certainly wasn't known in broader business circles. Without being able to put a name to it, I just felt like a fraud. I couldn't even articulate what it was that I was feeling, let alone devise a strategy to combat it. For quite some time, I simply stumbled through life with it weighing me down.

How did I eventually combat this crippling imposter syndrome? Well, I reached a stage in my career where, even though I knew I was on point with my instincts, I was still having trouble articulating business ideas and influencing colleagues or team members to turn my thoughts into action. I also felt I lacked confidence in making bigger, more important business decisions. I was a younger leader too — around 26 years old — so while I felt my instincts loud and clear, I did not yet have the confidence to trust them like I do now. I wish I would have, though, because looking back, every time I had strong instinct on something, it was perfectly on point.

I went to my amazing and thought-leading boss at the time and told him my dilemma. We discussed doing a short course at Auckland University, and I completed this a short time later. This course progressed into completing a three-year Master in Business Administration (MBA) degree. This turned out to be one of the best decisions I ever made.

Did the MBA help to allay my imposter syndrome? In part, yes. It gave me the confidence I desired to speak up and back myself. It taught me how to think critically, so I knew what I was saying had depth, intelligence and logic. However, the main driver in my journey to control imposter syndrome was a biennial reading (and putting its teachings into practice) of a book that has been a bible to me since the age of 23 — *Mind Power into the 21st Century* by John Kehoe. I just did not know at the first reading that this book was the answer to my plight.

You likely know the Buddhist phrase 'what you think, you become', or some other variation of this sentiment. Well, that sums up Kehoe's book. If you can control your thoughts, you can control imposter syndrome. Will it ever go away? Maybe, maybe not. But it can be controlled. I do feel, though, as we move into our forties that the amount of f*cks given does tend to dwindle, so perhaps it does get kicked to the curb eventually. However, through my corporate career in my twenties and thirties, I certainly had it in spades. So, if this is where you are at right now — 75 to 85 per cent of women are with you! My hope is that by realising your worth and building your leadership ability, you will be one of the women helping this statistic decline sharply in the coming years.

The antithesis of imposter syndrome: inner peace and confidence

Imagine, just for a moment, that you are looking at your life through someone else's eyes. What would they see? A well put-together woman who is articulate, smart, driven, strong, organised, kind, loving, a great friend, and an amazing mother? We need to find an inner peace from embracing these attributes and have confidence in them, rather than focusing on the things our mind conjures up as a mutated version of the truth, leading us to cut ourselves down before others have the opportunity to. Yes, I know. As a modern woman with a career, social life, maybe even a young family, you likely have a million things on the go, and you can feel downtrodden and exhausted — the opposite of those positive qualities just mentioned. But that is through your eyes, in your head. Again, I ask: what would someone else see? We are so full of kindness and love for everyone else, why not turn that attention to ourselves every once in a while?

PRODUCTIVITY TIP

List 10 positive attributes about yourself right now – grab a pen and paper or a device and physically write them out so you have them in front of you in black and white. Even if you do not fully believe them, list them anyway.

What did you come up with?

Tell yourself these attributes every day while waking up or as you drift off to sleep. During the day, be aware enough to catch yourself if you find you are sinking into a negative thought pattern, and replace those thoughts with one of your positive attributes, and just repeat it to yourself. Do this daily and you will be training your mind to control the type of thoughts you want to entertain.

Read *Mind Power into the 21st Century*. Better yet, read it every other year for the rest of your life. Doing so will keep more in check than just imposter syndrome. Your journey to realise your self-worth and your true value to others, supplemented with great resources that edify and uplift you (such as Kehoe's powerful book), is also the path to unlimited opportunity, and the charmed life you may currently feel is out of reach.

Everything I have truly wanted in my life has been achieved using the techniques in Kehoe's book. For the record, though, you do not get there by simply thinking about what you want, and it magically coming true — if that were the case, we would all be millionaires with model bodies. Sometimes when people put time and effort into visualisation and controlling their thoughts, the important step they often miss is taking action and walking through the metaphorical doors that open. This is called 'alignment'. You need to be consciously aware of your behaviour and actions, to ensure these align to your new way of thought. You will be surprised by how efficient and effective you can be when your visualisation and alignment come together.

I have many examples of using these techniques to my advantage — including achieving franchisee of the year in 2021, winning national dance competitions, getting my dream job, finding my perfect life partner and perfect house, even buying my dream car. Getting control of your thoughts is important. What you think, you become — whether those thoughts are good, bad or indifferent. Just remember to apply the action to those thoughts!

Enjoy your mind power journey — it is both liberating and fulfilling, and you'll be well on your way to combating your imposter syndrome.

Controlling your environment

Let me paint you a picture: You get up crazy early to get a jump on your emails before the household wakes and the morning routine kicks off. All too soon, you're deep in the kafuffle of kids not being able to find shoes, socks, uniform, lunchbox or homework. Or you're informed homework is due that previously you knew nothing about. God forbid 'book week' isn't sprung on you or an excursion you're only just finding out about. Pets to feed and walk, lunches to make, the list goes on. You finally get to work and commence the daily grind of back-to-back meetings from 9 am to 4 pm, whimpering through a couple of hepeating encounters. You leave the office or finish work around 5 pm and figure out what is for dinner on the way home based on your energy level and what happens to be in the fridge.

Sound familiar?

I did this (or something similar) for years.

While I loved my corporate career and I had clear passion and purpose, I was in overdrive a lot of the time. Always thinking of work or home and what I did or did not do or needed to do; it just didn't stop. A glass or three of wine did tend to help after my kid went to bed, but even then I woke up at 2 am, thinking through my checklist of the day ahead. I didn't realise how uptight I was until I compared how I am now with how I was then.

Now, let's talk about why understanding stress levels is important.

When we are in overdrive or a constant state of stress, we are constantly releasing cortisol throughout our bodies, which is our stress hormone. A little bit of cortisol is good because it keeps us alert and focused, but too much is bad. This leads to what is referred to as 'allostatic load', which is long-term wear and tear due to a chronic state of stress.

Too much cortisol running through your body for too long increases the neural connections to the part of the brain called the amygdala. The amygdala is a little almond-shaped part of your brain that's connected to the fight/flight/freeze response. Men typically have a larger amygdala than women, which some scientists believe explains the role of women as peacemakers in our ancient past. The amygdala enables your body to respond to a threat before conscious thought (that is, thought from the prefrontal cortex). In other words, you're responding before you really even understand what has happened. Say you're walking through bushes and see a snake. Your amygdala is what makes you jump out of the way before you can even rationalise what you are seeing.

If the neural pathways to your amygdala get stronger from the increased connections from too much cortisol, the hippocampus deteriorates. Your hippocampus has a major role in learning and long-term memory, but it's also a plastic and vulnerable structure that can get damaged by a variety of stimuli. So when the hippocampus weakens, so too does our ability to control stress — because your brain is quite literally shrinking and unable to regulate your behaviour from the stress triggers. Over time, the diminished parts of your brain can hamper your learning ability and also lead to chronic depression. The process can even affect your DNA — passing this on to future generations.

The hippocampus is definitely not an area we want to screw up if we can help it. Long-term regression of the hippocampus could eventually result in Alzheimer's disease. If you think about the way alcoholism results in damage to the liver due to years of alcohol abuse, the same can apply to stress leading to Alzheimer's — where the effect of chronic stress accumulates.

You can control your environment in lots of ways. One of them is by blocking out time during the day to ensure colleagues can't book you back-to-back. You can use this time for emails or just for thinking. Or maybe you can organise the kids' stuff the night before, so you can get some sand under your feet before the day starts. Perhaps it's simply getting the dog out for a walk, so he stops looking at you with those sad eyes that hold you to account in more ways than you care to admit. Controlling your day could also mean just saying the one word we say so much to ourselves, or our kids, but cannot seem to muster the ability to say it to other adults: 'no'. I don't need to teach you how to suck eggs here; ultimately, you know how to control your environment. What is more important to understand in this section is why you should.

Understanding your prefrontal cortex better (also covered in chapter 3) helps you to have more confidence to say 'no', and so avoid taking on too much. Also, understanding why you should limit multitasking ensures you are operating as productively as possible. This is because our brains can only really focus fully on one item at a time when performing a specific task. This increases to three or four when trying to decide between something or remember something — which is why we tend to chunk things such as phone numbers into three or four numbers at a time.

When trying to make a choice, we tend to only operate effectively when deciding between two or three things; anything more than this and it is easy to get into information overload. A state of feeling overwhelmed can affect our decision-making ability, sometimes stopping us from making decisions at all, and ultimately affecting our productivity or efficiency. It's so easy to be overwhelmed with too much information, especially in the social media world we live in today. Try to simplify life where you can, and give your brain a break.

Taking control of your environment is paramount to your success and wellbeing — otherwise, your environment will control you.

CHAPTER 2

VACAS
leadership styles

A quick online search can reveal the many leadership styles, methods and terms in circulation — offered by academics, business schools and journals or even individuals trying to make a quick buck. I've probably seen or heard about most of them, and no doubt you've seen a few yourself. However, after drawing on the learnings and insights I've gained throughout my career, I have settled on five leadership styles that have been key to my success. I have turned these leadership styles into the acronym VACAS — Visionary, Authentic, Coaching, Authoritative and Servant. As a leader, you need to have equal measures of VACAS, and you need to wear the different hats at different times, with different people, and in different circumstances.

However, the two styles you must have prior to engaging in any of the others are Authentic and Servant leadership. Without these, Visionary, Coaching and certainly Authoritative leadership are difficult to master, because trust and respect would not have been built to the required levels for high performance to take place. If staff don't trust you because they do not yet know you, or if you are seen to be hindering rather than helping, you will have a slow, uphill climb to get to your desired outcome — if you get there at all.

In this chapter, I've listed my VACAS leadership styles in the order of the acronym; however, feel free to jump ahead to the Authentic and Servant sections if you'd like more help in these areas first.

Visionary leadership

A Visionary leader cultivates inspiration by focusing on a long-term plan that they communicate to their employees impeccably. This naturally encourages a community of cohesive collaboration and teamwork.

Early on in my leadership career, I met someone who turned out to be one of the best bosses I have had the pleasure of working with. He was a true visionary, albeit in a sometimes-archaic industry that he unfortunately often had to battle from within. In the time that I was in his employ, he accomplished many great things, some of them market-leading firsts in New Zealand.

I was always enamoured by how he would present ideas and take you on a magical journey. He was a big-picture guy and no-one could fault his vision — inspiring and influencing people to rally behind him on these exciting journeys.

I learnt an important lesson while working for him: never underestimate the power of people's intrinsic motivations. For example, these motivations could be a sense of purpose, belonging, or working towards a mutual cause. When trying to motivate a team to do something, intrinsic motivation will always trump any carrot or stick methodology — for example, monetary reward for achievement (the carrot) or disciplinary action for non-achievement (the stick). This is a sentiment that Janine Allis, founder of Boost Juice, has echoed. Janine argues that everyone wants to do a good job, but how we motivate people to do that job varies. In her experience, that motivation is not always about money. (For more on Janine and Boost Juice, see the case study at the end of this part.)

Later in my career, I worked with my team on creating our department strategy — which became our five-year blueprint for the future. This plan detailed specific growth in markets we were going to target and what roles would be created as a result. We displayed this in very clear before and after organisational charts.

This strategy document did a couple of things:

1. Because it included before and after organisation charts, the team were given certainty that not only were their jobs safe — but they also had strong prospects for growth and career progression.

2. It created buy in and inclusivity on how this growth was going to eventuate. This created a strong sense of belonging and purpose.

As a result of this Visionary leadership, we were collectively very clear on where we were going, how long it was going to take to get there and, most importantly, how we were going to get there. We had clear vision, and an even clearer pathway. This bred motivation and loyalty and, therefore, sustainable high performance.

In summary, a Visionary leader in my VACAS model possesses these attributes:

- inspirational
- has a long-term plan
- excellent at communicating their long-term plan and bringing people on their journey.

Authentic leadership

An Authentic leader is transparent in both personality and business operations, making them easy to get to know and trust. Due to the greater trust and motivation this style inspires in employees, it also fosters a psychologically safe work environment — that is, an environment where staff can speak up, share ideas, ask questions and make mistakes without fear of humiliation or retribution. In other words, an environment where people thrive.

When I started in my leadership career, I had a small team consisting of just two customer service staff. When I got this promotion, I felt powerful and authoritative. I was outspoken and I was direct. I had little empathy—and I know this quantitatively. I started my MBA around the same time of this promotion and we were tested on empathy—and I tested low. Three years later, at the end of the MBA, two more leadership roles, and after having become a mother, I tested high. Empathy was an imperative leadership soft skill that I had learnt, over time.

I also lacked authenticity in my leadership role. I thought I had to be someone different in front of my staff than who I was normally. I was therefore inauthentic, and this created mistrust. I was a recipe for disaster and, while it was not a complete calamity, the culture I created as their leader was not always pleasant. Indeed, it was often tense, resulting in the team being unhappy or under-achieving—ironically, when happiness and high performance was what I desperately craved. Instead, I was getting the polar opposite. Recognising and acknowledging my leadership limitations and failings early on ended up being my saviour.

As the years progressed and I became more comfortable in my own skin as a leader, I stopped shying away from who I was. The person I was at work became very similar to the person I was at home—within reason. Life is just easier this way, too.

In the later years of my leadership career, I've enjoyed the other end of the spectrum. Since I have become unashamedly authentic with my staff, I have consistently had the most psychologically safe, and therefore highest performing teams, in the organisations in which I have worked. Even when mistakes were made, staff felt comfortable to speak up.

This also meant when less than ideal behaviours or results did happen and we needed to have those 'talks', the conversations were fluid, relatively relaxed, and usually ended on a high note. What is more, I did not have to beat around the bush with what I needed to say. Because we had built the relationship on trust, authenticity and respect, I could cut through the fluffy 'crap-sandwich' (where you start and end with something positive), and just say what needed to be said with love and care. I could keep the conversation light and even humorous at times — and, most importantly, productive.

PRODUCTIVITY TIP

Authenticity in leadership is not just about showing your personality and letting your staff get to know who you are. It is also about sharing what you need to do in the business to keep productivity high and not shying away from discussing aspects that could be relevant to your subordinates.

When humans feel like somebody is being inauthentic or that information is being kept from them, all sorts of uncertain feelings are conjured up and warning lights are going off in their mind — hampering productivity. Communicating future requirements is a balancing act, however; oversharing is not good either and I do believe in filtering out certain pressure cooker issues when communicating with staff so to not burden them, because this could stunt productivity.

When considering what to share with your staff, remember this: our brains crave certainty. The brain spends significant time each day trying to predict the future. Even a small amount of uncertainty generates an error response in the part of the brain known as the orbitofrontal cortex (OFC). This takes your attention away from the task at hand and focuses your attention on the error. Imagine this part of the brain as being like a car alarm going off when you're trying to concentrate on a particular task — it is very hard to ignore. The larger the amount of uncertainty — such as job insecurity or not knowing your boss's expectations — the more those alarms go off and the more productivity is affected.

As an example of how certainty can be created, I recently added some new services in my current business at Laser Clinics Australia. When considering each new service, and subsequently any new machines, required for my clinic, I made sure my managers and senior members of staff really understood the numbers involved in any potential purchase. For example, I shared with them capital expenditure (capex) costs and consumable costs, along with the market potential. We then built our targets and commission plans off this knowledge to ensure the launch of the new machine was going to be nothing but successful. Consequently, I had buy-in from the team, a very transparent commission structure, and a true understanding of the bottom line. The launch was so successful that within 10 days we had made our monthly target, and our clinic continues to do well nationally with the new services.

A significant change at work, such as a new revenue stream or service, can introduce feelings of unease if not managed well. Staff may wonder if their jobs are secure, if their earnings might be jeopardised, perhaps even if they are still capable or suited to the business. Using this change as an opportunity to create certainty instead of doubt bolsters a team's ability to perform—rather than having a team fragment due to the doubts and insecurities experienced by individual members of staff.

In summary, the Authentic leader in my VACAS model possesses these attributes:

- easy to get to know and trust

- creates psychologically safe environments for staff to excel in

- does not hold back relevant information.

Coaching leadership

Coaching leaders put the employee at the centre of their role and provide consistent parameters for staff to work within, assist with goal achievement and help remove any obstacles that may be encountered.

In each leadership role I held in my corporate career, I would sit face-to-face with each of my direct reports every week to do a 'one-to-one'. In our meeting, we would review the prior week's tasks and we would set up new tasks for the week ahead. Actionable tasks set in this meeting would filter through to their daily activities as appropriate for their role. Remember—humans like to be in control of their world, so I made sure that what were set as their tasks in these meetings came from them, not me.

Weekly tasks also needed to link to their quarterly key performance indicators (KPIs). Now whether you call them

KPIs or key success indicators (or any of the modern terms that are thrown around these days) is up to you. At the end of the day, KPIs are items that need to be achieved that link employee goals and tasks to the company's or the department's annual strategy. For a business's strategy to truly work, everything must link together — annual to quarterly, quarterly to monthly, monthly to weekly, weekly to daily. All strategies from all departments must interlink to ensure they are all running towards the same overarching goal. And all these strategies should link back to the backbone and soul of the business — its values.

I felt my job in these weekly one-to-one meetings was purely to steer conversations using the quarterly KPIs as our guiding light, so that the tasks my staff set for themselves for the week fed back to the achievement of their quarterly KPIs. I simply had to provide a consistent framework for them to work, and make decisions, within. Following our weekly one-to-one meetings, I gave them a printout of the tasks agreed to that would sit on their desk for them to physically tick off over the week.

Over the course of the week, I would check in with them on how they were going against the tasks and, as needed, help remove any hurdles or blockers they may have come up against, ensuring a clear pathway for their success. This process meant they were not just accountable to me; more importantly, they were accountable to themselves, and this was a much more powerful position to put them in.

In addition to the constant coaching through one-to-one meetings, I have always celebrated successes with my staff — especially new staff members, where acknowledging any quick wins helps boost confidence by making them feel accomplished early on. On the flip side, I have always engendered environments where speaking up about mistakes or experiences that did not quite go according to plan was equally as important as celebrating the successes. Continuous improvement and learning from mistakes are vital for growth.

Coaching leadership is about consistency. Taking small steps daily leads to the big achievements over the month, quarter or year. For more help in this area, I highly recommend the excellent book *Slight Edge* by Jeff Olsen.

In summary, the Coaching leader in my VACAS model possesses these attributes:

- understands the importance of providing consistent parameters for staff to work within

- constantly looks for ways to help remove hurdles staff may be facing and checks in regularly

- focuses on staff achieving their goals.

Authoritative leadership

Authoritative leadership is a management style most useful in pressure cooker situations where the leader needs to be in complete control to navigate through the issue at hand.

Out of the five leadership styles I promote in VACAS, this one is by far the most controversial. I do not condone authoritative leaders who get zero buy-in from staff in their daily interaction. Or leaders that dictate someone's day-to-day tasks, taking away their autonomy. However, this style does have a time and a place.

Under extreme pressure, or in extreme and urgent circumstances, it is okay for this style to trump others. Sometimes people do just need to be told what to do and how and when to do it. But this is only possible as a leader if you have first built respect and trust with your team through servant and authentic leadership — and I cannot stress this enough.

Picture this — even if you are not from a beauty services background, I'm sure you can relate. Imagine a laser clinic that is typically so busy it has five columns of client names in the booking system from 9 am to 7 pm. That's back-to-back 10- to 20-minute appointments per column — so an appointment book with at least 30 to 40 clients per column, per day. Now imagine the doors are about to open after a month-long COVID lockdown, and half an hour before opening you uncover a glitch in the system that meant none of the confirmation texts went out days earlier, meaning nobody was confirmed. Usually everyone is confirmed. You have five therapists rostered on, ready to do treatments — with potentially no clients coming. Disaster loomed.

I found myself in exactly this situation — and I was running around like a headless chicken, laptop under one arm, clipboard under the other, supporting and directing the team, as well as fending off centre management who were reprimanding us for having seats out front for clients (because we were not allowed more than five clients at any one time in the clinic due to COVID restrictions). After an intense hour or so — and orders being given left and right due to the time sensitive situation we found ourselves in — I witnessed the best example of teamwork that I have ever seen. By 10 am, we had reorganised an entire book of five rooms (difficult by anyone's standards), to have a fully booked (and confirmed) day ahead. Authoritative leadership in this situation worked.

The Authoritative leadership on display in this example used swift prioritisation under pressure and clear instructions directed to the staff on what needed doing and when. Because of the trust and respect within the team, there were no ruffled feathers, just a great display of teamwork in action.

Again, I do not condone daily Authoritative leadership; however, in situations where you have no other option but to (respectfully) bark orders, this style is a must to adopt. Again, this style is only possible, however, if you are standing on the servant- and authentic-leadership ground you have won.

In summary, the Authoritative leader in my VACAS model possesses these attributes in a pressure situation:

- excellent when communicating instructions
- excellent when prioritising
- excellent in an emergency.

Servant leadership

A Servant leader is humble and adapts the support they offer based on their staff's requirements. They put their employees' needs first with a focus on getting the very best out of their people.

Performing a few random acts of service for your staff is not enough to then consider yourself a servant leader. You must genuinely believe you are there to serve. Your job as leader is to remove hurdles for your people, and then get out of the way and let them flourish.

You will either naturally have servant leadership tendencies, or you won't. If you don't, that is okay. As with anything you need to work on, just be aware of your shortcomings and plug the necessary gaps so you become the best leader you can be for your people.

Leading from the front as well as leading from the back is a good way to depict servant leadership — providing whatever your staff require for them to feel supported. I remember when I was new in a leadership role and my team were unfamiliar with doing larger annual contract value (ACV) deals. Instead, the team were more used to deals that typically sat around $3000 ACV. Because I had the contacts and the knowhow, I uncovered a $20 000 ACV opportunity, and we worked on this together to bring it to life. I used both leadership from the front and from the back. In this case, the leadership from the front entailed leading by example, in showing team members how to uncover larger opportunities by bringing them into the process. My leadership from the back was displayed in letting team members then run with the deal, supporting their activity and guiding them to a successful conclusion — in which they received the recognition and financial benefit. After this, my team had broadened their thinking on what was available in their market and were upskilled to win larger ACV deals. This was a quick win to build my credibility with the team and it boosted their confidence too.

Servant leadership starts with you as the leader doing what you can for your staff, and sometimes that is not limited to within the workplace. I have done several things over the years that are a bit out of the ordinary, and definitely an extension into the real lives of team members and beyond the superficial interactions we can sometimes have at work. I have offered to pay the moving costs from Brisbane to the Gold Coast for a single mum, just to make her move easier. I have offered to have staff live at my house because they got caught up in a rental housing crisis. I have even offered to buy a cheap run-around car for a new starter, just so she could get to work and do her child drop-offs easily, because otherwise she had no way to buy it herself. I have also offered to buy a portable air conditioning unit so a staff member could get a decent night sleep in a hot Sydney summer.

So your servant leadership doesn't just come into play in work-related situations. In fact, sometimes offering ways to help someone out personally pays far more dividends than you could imagine. Not one of the staff members took me up on my offer, by the way, but they certainly knew I would have come through on it if they needed me to.

Servant leadership is genuinely caring about your team's welfare and them really feeling that. As managers and leaders, we wear different hats. Sometimes we are counsellors and sometimes we are coaches or cheerleaders. Your people should feel that they can come to you about anything — whether it is work-related or personal. These are the people who will stick by your side when the going gets tough and when you need them the most.

Servant leadership is also about gratitude. I am constantly grateful to my team for what they do. I appreciate the long hours they work and how they go above and beyond daily. I show them how grateful I am in many ways. One of these is the fun things we get to do as a team — shutting up shop for the day and chartering a boat for the afternoon, for example, or going to the best restaurant in the city for the evening of their lives.

Whatever you allow in your teams — good or bad — you will get back tenfold. There is one of you and many of them. Just be kind to people, show compassion, gratitude and care.

In summary, the Servant leader in my VACAS model possesses these attributes:

- bends over backwards for staff and thinks outside the square
- has a collaborative approach
- leads from the front and back.

VACAS inventory

The following VACAS inventory can help you identify where your natural leadership styles lie, and which styles you may need development in.

Simply go through each statement and tick to what level you agree, disagree or are neutral.

Be honest!

	Strongly disagree	Disagree	Neutral	Agree	Strongly agree
Visionary					
I am clear how my business will look two and five years into the future.					
I am clear on the values that would improve my business.					
I can think of several things that would motivate my team to perform better.					
I can identify challenging goals that should be focused on in my business.					
I can clearly articulate my business goals and values to my team.					
Authentic					
My friends and work colleagues would describe my personality the same way.					

	Strongly disagree	Disagree	Neutral	Agree	Strongly agree
My staff freely come to me when they've made mistakes, without fear of retribution.					
I share all relevant business information with my staff.					
I admit my mistakes to others.					
My morals guide what I do as a leader.					
Coaching					
I create an environment for my team to share experiences and use these as learning opportunities.					
I remove hurdles for staff to enable them to flourish.					
I actively focus on professional growth in my team.					

(continued)

	Strongly disagree	Disagree	Neutral	Agree	Strongly agree
I look for coachable moments throughout the day.					
My role is to provide an encouraging and consistent environment for my staff to work within, so they can accomplish their objectives.					
Authoritative					
I like to give orders to ensure everyone knows their place.					
I am the judge of the achievements of the members in my team.					
Most employees feel insecure about their work and need direction.					

	Strongly disagree	Disagree	Neutral	Agree	Strongly agree
As a rule, staff must be given rewards or punishments in order to motivate them to achieve organisational objectives.					
Staff need to be supervised closely and given direction throughout the day.					
Servant					
My staff often seek help from me for a personal problem.					
I make the career development of my staff a priority.					
I like to collaborate with my team to get the best strategies in place.					

(continued)

	Strongly disagree	Disagree	Neutral	Agree	Strongly agree
I understand the importance of leading from the front and back.					
I put the best interests of others above my own.					

Where did you get the most ticks in 'strongly agree'? Where did you get the most in 'strongly disagree'? What is your natural leadership style? Where could you round out your leadership toolkit with some development?

 **PRODUCTIVITY TIP**

You probably don't want to test high in Authoritative Leadership – but it is important that you can be authoritative in high pressure situations.

CHAPTER 3
Understanding your brain for effective leadership

I appreciate it may seem a little random to have a full chapter about the brain in a business book. However, bear with me, because without this knowledge, I would not have become the leader I am today.

Knowledge about the brain has enabled me to take almost a cookie-cutter approach to staff and teams, rather than going down rabbit holes of understanding each person individually and psychologically. So I don't need to go as deep as to find out what happened to little Jimmy on the playground when he was five years old, for example, to understand why he holds a particular bias as a 40-year-old man today that is stunting his creativity or growth at work. Honestly, who has time to get that deep with every staff member? Peeling back the layers of the onion until you figure out the problem lies in Jimmy's five-year-old self? No thanks. People have much more appropriate ways to dig into their individual psychology, with the help of professionals, family or friends.

A workplace perfectly tailored to every individual is impossible to achieve, and would be counterproductive anyway. Applying an understanding of how our brains generally drive behaviour, however, is a simple way to create a workplace culture of safety and high performance.

Let's start with some fun facts about the brain to lighten up this topic:

- Your brain is just 2 per cent of your body mass but requires 20 per cent of your total oxygen consumption. The more you can boost your oxygen intake, the better, because this enables you to think clearer. (This is one of reasons exercise is so good for us — it sends more oxygen into the brain.)

- Our brains consist of about 80 per cent water.

- Size wise, our brains are about the size of a grapefruit.

- If you've ever tried cocaine (or even if you haven't), perhaps you've wondered how the drug works in the body. Well, cocaine blocks the brain's ability to get rid of the neurotransmitters that detect you are tired, which means they pool, making you feel 10 feet tall and bulletproof — for about 10 minutes anyway.

- Ever drive to work and genuinely not remember how you got there? You can thank the part of your brain called the basal ganglia for that. It is a nifty part of the brain that we can rely on when performing the tasks we don't have to consciously think about — for example, driving a car, flushing the toilet, putting the garage door down and locking the front door. If you cannot remember doing these things, don't worry — your basal ganglia 100 per cent have your back.

To understand how our brains function, there are three key principles:

1. The brain's key role is to keep us safe. We are either in an approach (reward) state, or an avoidance (threat) state. For productivity to be at its best, we need to keep ourselves and our staff in the approach/reward state. I discuss the approach and avoidance states in more detail in the 'Fight/ flight/freeze' section later in this chapter. And in chapter 4, I discuss the SCARE model, which is your tool to keeping staff in the reward/ approach state.

2. Your brain is a predication organ. You spend half your waking hours predicting what will happen — whether you are conscious of it or not.

3. You brain tries to conserve energy wherever possible. Your brain conserves energy to keep this energy in store to deal with threats in your environment.

Hormones and neurotransmitters: Your brain's messengers

Hormones and neurotransmitters are your body's messengers from the brain, transmitting information around the body based on what you are experiencing or feeling in that moment. The neurotransmitters and hormones detailed in the following sections contribute to maintaining high productivity.

Dopamine

Dopamine, in short, is responsible for our arousal in learning. When we find something interesting, dopamine is being released. This produces a reward state of mind. Dopamine and novelty go hand in hand. Social media is rife with dopamine hits — from every 'like' on Facebook or Instagram, to every view on YouTube or TikTok.

An important point to note here is that, while we think we are being productive when we multitask, all we are doing is creating a dopamine addiction feedback loop. We are simply rewarding the brain for losing focus and for constantly searching for external stimulation. Believe it or not, multitasking creates greater cognitive loss than smoking a joint.

Oxytocin

Oxytocin is our love hormone. From a work perspective, even having similar interests to someone else releases oxytocin. When you feel like you have something in common with somebody you have just met, or when you are introduced to someone through a mutual friend, oxytocin is more likely to be present. This allows for people to be more engaged with each other, and have more trust which translates to higher productivity.

PRODUCTIVITY TIP

When you hire a new staff member, buddy them up with someone from day one. This enables them to build stronger connections and settle in quicker, allowing for your team's productivity to increase faster.

Endorphins

Endorphins are released by your brain during pleasurable activities such as exercise, massage, eating and (yes) sex. They're also released when your body feels pain and are its natural pain killer. Endorphins:

- counteract cortisol (the stress hormone)
- reduce blood pressure
- stimulate the immune system
- relax tense muscles.

Serotonin

Serotonin is the hormone responsible for your good moods and, when we are in a good mood and have a more positive outlook, we are able to make better decisions, solve problems, and be more productive. The best way to boost serotonin levels is through a good night's sleep — and the best way to achieve that is through exercise and a good diet.

In chapter 2 I discuss Servant leadership, and I mention a staff member who was not getting enough sleep because he didn't have an air conditioning unit in his apartment. He was not productive at work due to this issue. An easy fix in my mind was to offer to buy a portable unit so he could get the sleep he needed. An understanding of what the brain and body need to be productive can put you in a position where you can positively influence your staff's workplace productivity, while practising good leadership.

Epinephrine

Epinephrine is the neurotransmitter behind the body's fight/flight/freeze response. This neurotransmitter effectively gets our body ready for action and lasers in our focus, making us feel 'wired'. Therefore, it is most dormant when we sleep. This is a great neurotransmitter when it gets going because it makes us super productive!

Cortisol

I discuss cortisol in chapter 1, so I don't cover it in any detail here. The main aspect to keep in mind is that cortisol is your stress hormone. A little cortisol is great — it keeps you on your toes, alert and focused. A lot of it constantly running through your body, however, can do serious damage to your mental health and the hippocampus in your brain.

Triune versus Adaptive Brain theory

In the 1960s, neuroscientist Paul MacLean proposed his Triune Brain model, arguing that our brains have three key regions of functionality, and that these three areas developed and evolved over time.

In MacLean's model, the three key regions are as follows:

1. The reptilian brain, responsible for regulating heart rate, temperature, sucking and breathing.

2. The emotional brain (that is, the limbic system), came second and is responsible for our automatic motivation and emotional responses.

3. The neocortex was the last to evolve, and is responsible for higher cognitive thought, language and decision-making.

The Triune Brain model was largely accepted throughout academia and is referred to in many coaching and leadership discussions. However, this model is now being challenged by modern scientists. Neuro-evolutionists now argue that the brain growing or developing into each region over thousands of years of evolution is unlikely. Rather, they argue that all areas of the brain were likely always there, and that our brains have instead adapted to our changing environments. The neuroscience community now largely agrees that the brain does not function independently of its structures, such as the way MacLean's Triune Brain model suggested, but works together in a solar system of synapses and connections, utilising valuable real estate in the brain if it is otherwise unused.

As an example of this, in 2011 neuroscientists Eleanor Maguire and Katherine Woollett published their findings after studying London taxi driver trainees over the four years it took to acquire their licence. (Known as 'The Knowledge', London taxi drivers must memorise a labyrinth of 25 000 streets within a 10-kilometer radius of Charing Cross train station, as well as thousands of tourist attractions and hot spots.) Through using magnetic resonance imaging (MRI), Maguire and Woollett were able to show that the hippocampus (responsible for long-term memory) had grown larger in these taxi drivers' brains due to their enormous memory bank of the roads of London. (This was before having Google Maps on our phones.) The hippocampus had taken over other parts of the brain (unused real estate) to grow to the size it did to bank all those memories. The correct term for this example of the taxi drivers' brains changing is 'neuroplasticity'. Fascinating stuff!

The Adaptive Brain model, developed by Patrick Steffen, Dawson Hedges and Rebekka Matheson (and outlined in their 2022 article 'The brain is adaptive not triune: How the brain responds to threat, challenge, and change'), specifically challenges the Triune Brain model. Steffen, Hedges and Matheson assert that our brains are adaptive and will constantly reflect what is going on inside us (our emotional responses to stimuli) and external to us (our perception of situations we find ourselves in, or our environment). The brain's continuous and overarching goal of keeping us safe is carried out by it making predictions of what will happen next time we encounter a certain stimuli or environment. Our brains are then constantly assessing new information coming in, and ordering this information in such a way as to minimise any prediction errors when determining the best course of action. Our brain never switches off—even when we are sleeping or resting, sophisticated connections are in play.

To contextualise this, when you hire a new person, the stimuli and environment they experience is often nervousness and uncertainty, respectively. However, as the synapses in their brain build the required bridges to encode new memories, eventually this new staff member's brain will minimise the prediction errors and feel safer. When they move away from the threat status and towards the reward state of mind, they can also more easily adopt company systems and processes, and settle into the social norms. This is why the buddy system works so well when a new person starts.

The Adaptive Brain model also works off the theory that our brains are highly interconnected, rather than consisting of fairly independent structures working separately depending on the issue at hand, as the Triune Brain model had earlier suggested.

The remarkable prefrontal cortex

The prefrontal cortex, located just behind the forehead, accounts for around 10 per cent of our brains, and is just one part of the overall neocortex (introduced in the previous section). The prefrontal cortex is responsible for holding the contents of your conscious thought at any one time; however, it is relatively inefficient at keeping the copious amounts of thoughts and other stimuli that come in each day in order.

The prefrontal cortex oversees your goal setting and controls your impulses — and that one's kind of important. Otherwise, if you suddenly felt hot, you might strip off your clothes and run around naked. It is the proprietor of problem-solving and thinking creatively. But it only has limited space to function productively.

Another factor at play here is that our brains are more visual rather than linguistic. This, combined with the limited space available in your prefrontal cortex, has many implications in the workplace and for you as a leader. For example, if you have lots of tasks or thoughts in your mind, it is important to get them out of your head onto a whiteboard or piece of paper — draw pictures if you need to. Spend a few minutes looking at what you've written down and drawn, and then prioritise. As a leader, it is also important to watch out for people who seem to have lots on their plate all the time, or those who don't naturally prioritise well — they could be at risk of being overwhelmed or burning out.

To operate efficiently, our prefrontal cortex requires the right amount of glucose and oxygen to fuel it. So you need to always try to increase oxygen to the brain, because this optimises your ability to problem-solve and think clearly. If you need to have a serious conversation, for example, do it standing up or walking because this immediately provides 15 per cent more blood to your brain. This means 15 per cent more oxygen and glucose, which increases the brains efficiency. Every 30 minutes, get up and go for a walk because this will help you to remain focused.

When we are in a threat state, on the other hand, oxygen is drawn away from our prefrontal cortex and into the emotional connections of the brain (specifically, the amygdala). This creates that adrenaline rush you feel when someone just makes you angry or stresses you out, for example. It is your body's response to get ready for fight or flight. When this happens, you literally do not have the oxygen in your working memory (prefrontal cortex) to think logically or problem-solve.

The prefrontal cortex is a remarkable organ; however, as mentioned, it is a very inefficient processor. You could liken it to 10 chefs running around a commercial kitchen making one bowl of soup. Unless you exercise control over your prefrontal cortex (aka your conscious thoughts) and be disciplined, these thoughts are just going to go everywhere at once because distractions are all too easy! And this has a negative effect on your thinking and problem-solving. As an example of this, a University of London study showed that constantly being distracted by email or text messaging reduces mental capability by an average of 10 IQ test points — five for women and 15 for men. The effect was similar to losing a night's sleep.

Again, *Mind Power into the 21st Century* by John Kehoe (which I mention in chapter 1) is a valuable resource here, because it helps you take back the rightful control of the thoughts in your head.

If you want to master productivity in the workplace and achieve consistent and sustainable high-performing teams, a sound understanding of the prefrontal cortex is vital to your success. I also recommend *Your Brain at Work* (2009) by Dr David Rock. This book takes a deep dive into this topic in a fun, relatable and metaphoric way.

Fight/flight/freeze

As mentioned already, one of the entire organising principles of your brain is to keep you safe — that is, minimising threat and maximising reward. You and your team remaining in a reward state is vital for problem-solving and to remain productive. So your job as leader is to focus on maximising this reward state, so you can get the best out of your people, constantly.

Our threat responses of fight/flight/freeze are often bubbling away just below the surface and can be easily triggered. However, as I introduce here and discuss in much more detail in the next chapter, models are available to help you avoid triggering threat responses and so keep yourself and your team in a reward state of mind, ensuring sustained and optimised productivity.

Another way to think about the threat verses reward state is to use a model developed by Linda Ray, founder and CEO of NeuroCapability — a leadership training provider that applies the latest in cognitive and social neuroscience to leadership, psychological safety and wellbeing. Ray's model replaces the words 'threat' and 'reward' with 'protective mode' verses 'productive mode' and shows this as a continuum. Effectively, when your staff are in protective mode, they are less likely to take accountability for any mistakes or take any risks, and their attention is focused inwards on themselves instead of looking holistically to problem solve. Conversely, if your staff are in productive mode, they feel safe enough to take risks and make mistakes, and are always looking outwards to solve problems collaboratively.

Let me give you an example from a time in my career when I was in protective mode. I was in the middle of my management career, and I had a boss who was intimidating, to say the least. He could be a barrel of laughs, too, and awesome company. But when he was in a mood, everyone knew about it, even people on the other side of the building. Let's just say, in terms of star signs, he was a typical Leo.

In one particular instance, he came storming into my office, demanding to know answers on a current project. He was a big man too — I'm not so short myself at 5'9' but, in that moment, he towered over me. Luckily, I had recently learned about what happens to the prefrontal cortex when you're put under extreme pressure. This meant I knew the reason I couldn't think of the answers wasn't because I did not know them; it was because my body was reacting to the physiological stress he was putting me under. My threat/ protection status was screaming internally, so the oxygen I required in my prefrontal cortex to provide the answers was swiftly dispersed into my extremities — under the orders of the amygdala via epinephrine — to enable my fight/flight/ freeze response.

Knowing and understanding this, I mustered up the only response I could think of (in my state of limited thinking capacity) and said, 'I will come and see you in your office with the answer when *you* have calmed down.' Within ten minutes or so of him having stormed in, and then out, of my office, the answer naturally popped into my head, and I went and told him what he needed to know. Better than that, he also apologised.

Being in a fight or flight mode affects the part of our central nervous system called the sympathetic nervous system. When this happens, we have certain physiological responses — including a dry mouth, surges of adrenaline, dilated pupils and accelerated heartbeat. At its most extreme, the hormones released while in threat status disrupt the usual hormones that keep the bladder relaxed, causing bladder contraction — which is why some people can pee their pants when scared witless.

Conversely, when we realise the threat was a false alarm and start to calm down, our parasympathetic nervous system kicks in and we move into the 'rest and repair' state. When this happens, our physiological responses include slower heartrate, constricted pupils, stimulated saliva and relaxed bladder. In essence, the parasympathetic and sympathetic nervous systems are on a continuum, and we move between the two based on our reactions to our environments and subsequent emotions.

Both sympathetic and parasympathetic are controlled by two glands: the hypothalamus and the pituitary.

At all times possible, you want to keep yourself and your team in an approach/reward/productive state, because being in this state is closely linked to positive emotions and increased dopamine levels — vital for interest and learning. When people are in the reward state, they are 50 per cent more likely to be able to problem-solve. Moreover, a large and growing amount of research indicates that people who experience positive emotions perceive more options when trying to solve problems, can solve nonlinear problems that require more insight, and collaborate more effectively to generally perform better overall.

Staying in this state, and ensuring your prefrontal cortex is functioning optimally, actually has a lot in common with Goldilocks (yes, from the 19th-century fairytale). Both must have everything just right. This is a useful analogy used widely in the academic world, and one to be mindful of when putting the model outlined in the next chapter — SCARE — into practice.

CHAPTER 4

SCARE: An organisational neuroscience leadership model

After going through countless leadership offsites and training days, and completing an MBA, I discovered a framework that I believe stands head and shoulders above the rest when it comes to effective leadership strategies. This is the SCARE model, developed by Linda Ray, founder and CEO of NeuroCapability (introduced in the previous chapter). It is the only framework I have come across in my career that genuinely provides a sweet spot to work within that keeps people in a reward state of mind, ensuring productivity is optimised and gives you the best chance at higher rates of staff longevity.

In this chapter, I outline what SCARE is and explain each of the domains in the acronym. In addition, I provide some contextualised anecdotal stories, and examples of how the reward and threat status is triggered.

The five domains of the SCARE model are Significance, Certainty, Autonomy, Relatedness and Equity.

All sane humans living in a society operate in all five domains — but not necessarily in equal measure. We generally have higher needs in one or two specific domains. For example, I have high needs in Significance and Autonomy. A domain's importance can also change over the course of your life. When we are in our twenties, for example, we may have high needs for Certainty, and this may change to Autonomy as we mature. The importance of different domains may also change in different environments or circumstances.

Each domain's threat trigger can be bubbling away just under the surface, so your responsibility as a leader is to make sure you are creating environments where everyone in your team has the best chance of remaining in the 'reward' state, optimising productivity.

As I mention in the previous chapter, think Goldilocks and getting everything 'just right'.

Significance

The Significance element of the SCARE model focuses in on people's sense of importance and where they fit with others in a social context — and humans care about this a lot. This is likely a derivative from our cave-dwelling days where knowing our place in the pecking order was about literal survival. These days, your staff want to feel they make a significant contribution at work. As figure 4.1 shows, this Significance can be threatened or rewarded.

| **S** SIGNIFICANCE (our relative importance to other people) | **Threat activators** • titles and formal power • belittling • feeling disconnected from the goals of the organisation • critical feedback | **Reward activators** • acknowledgement • recognising strengths • appreciation of contribution • asking for input/expertise • public positive feedback |

Figure 4.1 Significance threat and reward activators
Source: NeuroCapability

Significance can be threatened very easily, such as by challenging or dismissing an idea a colleague puts forward, taking credit for an idea that was not yours, or even just saying to a colleague or subordinate something like, 'If I were you...' or 'Can I offer you some advice?' You may already have an example that has popped into your head when your Significance felt triggered.

As adults, we are very well trained in hiding our triggers due to our rational connections in our brain being fully developed. So while you as the leader may not see a threat response from a staff member outwardly, this doesn't mean they didn't have a physiological response that has now put them in a threat state. Unfortunately, being in this state shuts off their productivity—until either they, or you, pull them back over to the reward state. Of course, with a lot of our meetings still being held online (via platforms such as Zoom) since the COVID-19 pandemic, picking up on a person's threat status can be harder than ever. Never underestimate the power of face-to-face communication with your team, especially for any feedback-style discussions. You can often pick up on much more if you are in front of someone, rather than communicating through a computer screen or, worse, phone or, even worse still, text or email.

PRODUCTIVITY TIP

When having the 'feedback' conversation with a staff member or colleague, ask that person to provide feedback about themselves first, and then have an open and engaged conversation.

Significance is about relative importance. According to researcher Professor Michael Marmot, the more important you feel, the less the cortisol levels in your system, the heathier you are, and the longer you live. A threat to Significance can generate a strong threat response and, interestingly, lights up the same part of your brain as physical pain. If you have ever been dumped, if you think back to that moment, perhaps you can also remember the physical pain like no other in your heart from being heartbroken.

We all have a desire to feel we are contributing to something meaningful, so clearly communicating how tasks contribute to the business purpose can provide a sense of purpose and motivation in your people, especially if their values align with your own, your business and/or your department. Also, when was the last time you showed appreciation and gave thanks to the people in your workplace? And not just your own staff, but others across the business?

⏱ PRODUCTIVITY TIP

Showing appreciation and giving thanks is such a simple and under-utilised strategy that can easily create a reward state in people and stimulate great productivity.

As an example of being in a Significance reward state, I clearly remember how I felt when I received a promotion that was to move me from Auckland, New Zealand, to Sydney, Australia. I stayed in that reward state for months due to the public recognition of my consistent hard work, determination and success in the role in New Zealand.

Conversely, a major triggering of a Significance threat status that hit me hard in my early leadership career was when senior management made the tough decision to take out the middle managers through a restructure—which meant my role was made redundant. I understand why that had to be done now but, at the time, I was devastated. It was a hard pill to swallow and affected me for a good while before I bounced back, but bounce back I did.

Certainty

Our brains spend significant time trying to predict the future. Of the 70 000 thoughts we have on average every day, scientists estimate that around 42 per cent are focused on trying to predict what might happen in the future. For this reason, our brains crave certainty—which is a real challenge, given the constant change we often experience in the workplace.

Figure 4.2 highlights the kinds of things that can affect Certainty in your staff.

CERTAINTY
(seeking predictability)

Threat activators
• unclear expectations
• constantly changing goal posts
• turning up late to meetings

Reward activators
• clear roles
• known timeframes
• specific agendas

Figure 4.2 Certainty threat and reward activators
Source: NeuroCapability

You need to give your staff as much certainty as possible, so be clear about your expectations, clarify the next steps, and outline roles and boundaries in order to maintain high productivity levels.

Mapping out development plans and openly talking about growth enables staff to know how they fit into strategy plans, which increases the reward circuitry. Be as transparent as possible. Agree how long a meeting will run for, for example, and state clear objectives at the start of any discussion.

 PRODUCTIVITY TIP

Set expectations and give your people any information relevant for them to do their roles, even if you're communicating something uncertain such as a restructure. Providing certainty on the dates staff will know an outcome of the restructure will ensure your best chance of maintaining productivity.

When deciding what I wanted to do after I relocated to the Gold Coast, I knew I wanted to be my own boss; however, I knew the security of a decent salary was very important to me also. This guided my decision of becoming a franchisee in the Laser Clinics Australia franchise network — because this allowed me to run my own business but also provided the certainty of knowing where my next pay was coming from. This kept me in a reward state and ensured my own productivity was optimised while I was heavily focused on building the business in the first 18 months.

COVID lockdowns and the state border closures in Australia threw everything I knew about reward states in Certainty out of the window. My business is located in New South Wales but very close to the Queensland–New South Wales border. However, 30 per cent of my clients and the majority of my staff, including myself, lived in Queensland, so the closures affected the business significantly. For a long while, we had no certainty, and this generated strong threat responses almost daily. On the flip side, the situation helped build resilience, for both myself and my staff.

Autonomy

The third domain in the social world we pay attention to is our intense need for Autonomy. Do you like being instructed on what to do with little input? Neither do I! On the other hand, when we feel we have choice and influence, we're much more likely to enter a reward state. Providing more Autonomy can be as simple as asking a staff member which issue they (or the team) should tackle first, or what they think is the best approach in a specified situation.

Figure 4.3 highlights the Autonomy factors that can lead to either a reward or threat state.

AUTONOMY	Threat activators	Reward activators
(our perception of control over events)	• command and control • 'If I were you ..' • 'You should ..' • micromanaging	• a sense of choice • being allowed to find solutions • a sense of ownership over jobs or tasks

Figure 4.3 Autonomy threat and reward activators
Source: NeuroCapability

In particular, micromanaging is a killer for Autonomy and generates significant threat in the brain. If your staff feel micromanaged or unheard, they also feel they have an inability to influence outcomes, and this can generate a strong threat response. It is important for your staff to feel they have control over their environment — to have choices.

Using kids as an example here is a really easy way to drive this point home. When trying to get my preschooler dressed in the morning, I would never give him just one option for his tee-shirt or shorts. Instead, I would always give him a choice between two for each item, which would give him a sense of control over his environment. Due to this simple strategy, we would usually have fairly stress-free mornings. I used the same approach for anything I wanted him to do — for example, 'Do you want to go to bed at 7.20 or 7.30?', 'Should we leave for school at 8.20 or 8.30?' or 'Do you want 10 or 15 more minutes on the TV?' Providing this perceived sense of autonomy saved many debates. Adults in workplaces, to a certain level, are no different. They also want options, and certainly don't want to be dictated to.

An important point to remember here, however, is that while people want Autonomy, you also need to ensure they feel they have the competence and skills necessary to do a task. Without this, you can easily move your people into a threat state. You need to make sure you match a task or project with a person's level of competence (more on this in chapter 6).

PRODUCTIVITY TIP

Ensure you have pathways in place for your staff to build competence and skill, because this is key to keeping people engaged and productivity maintained.

When setting up a stakeholder agreement back when I was in the property industry, it was important to me that I remained in an autonomous position within the business. We therefore structured the shareholding in such a way that my Autonomy was protected, thus allowing my reward state to continue for optimised focus and productivity.

Early in my leadership career, I had an interim manager put in place after our CEO left. This interim manager — let's call him Rick (with a silent 'P') — generated the worst threat response I have ever had in my career in terms of my Autonomy. This not only stunted my productivity but, worse, also temporarily shattered my confidence.

Although my results in this role were the best in the country, and I juggled these results with completing my MBA,

I was instructed by Rick that I must give up the study to focus only on the role. I completed the MBA work outside of work hours, so this just made no sense, especially since I was already fulfilling every part of my role. The sheer unfairness of having my choices taken away and feeling boxed into an unjustified corner was too much to bear.

Office bullying, or 'office politics' as we called them back then, also hit me like a tonne of bricks whenever I went into the office. The whole situation had turned toxic and it was an awful place to be. I had worked too hard to just give up the MBA and I was clearly no longer in alignment with the company or the new interim manager, so my only option was to leave, which is what I did. This was heartbreaking at the time because I had built a reputable name in the industry and was passionate about what we did. But it's always important to remember that you don't have to stay in a role — you always have other options, and absolutely nothing is worth feeling miserable in your day-to-day job. It is just not worth it. No-one goes to their grave wishing they worked more!

And, of course, an MBA is a fantastic and complementary degree as you work on developing your corporate leadership career, and not something to be given up on a whim. Why Rick felt he had to box me in to that corner can only be answered by him (but I have my suspicions).

Relatedness

We are all born to connect, and we want to feel part of a social group. This forms part of our Relatedness to other people.

We crave entry into a tribe of like-minded people — referred to as our 'in group' or our 'tribe'. However, our brains treat every new person we meet as foe before friend — until we identify something about the other person that is like us. Our brains defaulting to seeing others as foe first links back to when we lived in caves and clans and this was essential for our survival. When a stranger came onto our land, they could pose a real threat and, as such, we treated each person as a potential threat. Again, our brain's number one goal is to keep us safe so unknown people will always be foes before friends. Indeed, meeting people who are unknown to us can generate a threat response.

Running along this tendency to be wary of 'outsiders' is a strong desire to connect with those we see as 'insiders' — to form groups and teams to feel a sense of belonging. Safe human contact is a primary driver according to neuroscientist Professor John Cacioppo, similar to the need for food. Absence of this can generate the threat response of feeling lonely. This is why we feel better at a party knowing three people rather than one or, worse still, none.

Figure 4.4 highlights how Relatedness can affect the reward and threat states.

RELATEDNESS (our connectedness to those around us)	**Threat activators**	**Reward activators**
	• social exclusion • not looking at a person when addressing a team	• connecting with others • checking in • spending time with people you enjoy

Figure 4.4 Relatedness threat and reward activators
Source: NeuroCapability

To find a common connection with someone releases oxytocin (discussed in chapter 3). If two people or a group of people have a great affiliation, this will produce more oxytocin. Feeling a sense of Relatedness with someone is closely linked to trust.

PRODUCTIVITY TIP

The greater staff members trust each other, the stronger the collaboration and the more information that is shared, which results in higher productivity. So find a way to connect over something in common with your team to build trust quickly, especially in a new environment.

When I started in one of my senior leadership positions, discovering that one of my new subordinates was from the same small town I was helped greatly—and even more so when I found out he just happened to be friends with my mother, with whom I was very close. He quickly became a 'buddy' and made my entire settling in period full of warmth and great energy. Through being in this reward state, we were able to turn this energy into productivity very quickly.

This was in stark contrast to a national advisory board I had to join later in my leadership career. The sole purpose of this board was to extract ideas from each of the members to improve business operations, and we were obliged to participate in a three-hour Zoom call each quarter. These meetings provided limited opportunity to produce anything remotely close to oxytocin being released. Several members appeared to already be friends rather than foes and any ideas that were shared by outsiders were often shot down. Whether intentionally or not, these responses put us 'outsiders' in a threat state. Needless to say, this foe/threat state remained, and productivity in those meetings was bleak.

Equity

We all want to feel we are being treated fairly and equitably. This is our sense of Equity, and we often measure our sense of fairness against the treatment of others — looking at, for example, whether others in the team are getting the better jobs or projects, or are being rewarded more than us. The minority/gender pay gap creates a huge amount of unfairness for many marginalised people, as an example.

When we experience a threat to fairness, we can lose perspective and act in ways that make no sense to those around us, or sometimes even ourselves. As a leader, you need to be mindful of how easy it is to cause a threat in this particular domain, because a threat in one domain can have a domino effect in the others.

Figure 4.5 outlines how the Equity factor can be influenced.

EQUITY (perception of a fair deal; transparency)	**Threat activators**	**Reward activators**
	• unequal treatment of self or others • reward structures that seem to favour particular people	• sharing work equally • check for fairness • ensuring decision-making is transparent

Figure 4.5 Equity threat and reward activators
Source: NeuroCapability

The intrinsic human need for fairness explains why we experience internal reward for doing volunteer work. Unfair exchanges, on the other hand, often generate a very strong threat response and can activate the insular cortex — a part of the brain involved in intense emotions such as disgust. A feeling of unfairness is what drives us to protest (which we saw a lot of throughout the COVID lockdowns and vaccination arguments).

Reducing the threat for your staff and increasing the reward circuits of feeling equitable can be as simple as increasing transparency and the level of communication. Establishing clear expectations and setting of ground rules can also increase a sense of fairness. Because this domain stimulates such an intense emotion, it is always useful to ask yourself, 'Is this fair?' That is, is this fair on the company, fair on your teammates, fair on your staff and fair on yourself? You should be able to answer this before making any decisions.

In the introduction, I mention the guardian angel who cleared my debt after I had to take a former employer to court. Three months after starting in my new role with this guardian angel, he was so pleased with what I had accomplished that he gave me a significant pay rise. While I was not expecting a rise of that level, I knew I had produced significant process and procedure improvements within the business, as well as strong sales results. My guardian angel, therefore, considered this to be a fair exchange. My sense of fairness — my Equity factor — was deeply set in the reward state for a long time due to this, which enabled my high-performance productivity to continue.

I learnt from this boss that paying people that little bit more takes the issue of money off the table, allowing them to focus on the tasks at hand. Within reason, as a leader you should always find ways to pay your staff bonuses, rather than look for ways to not pay them (as can sometimes be the case in the corporate world).

Furthermore, I never understood managers who set targets too high or made them unachievable — sometimes even out of reach of the very highest of performers. Targets should be a stretch but should never be unachievable. Often unrealistic and unachievable targets are the result of a manager higher up who has simply accepted the fate of having these targets handed down from their own bosses. If that happens to you, have the courage to fight for your team. If you know the targets are not realistic, your staff will too, no matter how you try to sell it to them. They'll feel they're being treated unfairly, and that you don't care about Equity. Instead, fight for them — that is your job. How do you expect to create a team of trust and psychological safety — and, therefore, high performance — if you do not have their backs? Targets being set too high for what is a reasonable expectation of effort will completely stunt productivity, because all motivation would be lost. As I said, targets should absolutely be a stretch, but never out of reach.

My experience while working with 'Rick' (see the 'Autonomy' section, earlier in this chapter) produced a domino of threat responses in not just my Autonomy but also my sense of Equity. I remember one particular meeting with Rick, when I was already apprehensive about going into the office due to the 'office politics' in play. During the meeting Rick, accused me of not doing anything productive while 'out in the field' and asked me to explain myself. This choice of management style put me on the defensive and gave me cause to feel doubt and confusion. The general perception in the business was that my activity levels were strong, and my revenue figures were to be applauded. My targets were consistently achieved and, at 55 per cent over the set target, were the highest out of all the field managers. Feedback from my customers had been outstanding on customer service issues. I also felt I was providing support to the sales team when they needed it, in addition to my designated responsibilities.

Overall, the feedback from everyone I had formed relationships with across the country over my four years with the organisation, along with the growth of my own territory, suggested that I was having a significant impact on the success of the business at that time. However, the powerful disconnect I observed from Rick between my achievements and abilities and his perception of the situation caused me to feel attacked, defeated and intimidated. It felt, simply, unfair.

At this point, my confidence shattered. I was forced to question my understanding of my actual and perceived place within the company and, what was worse, I started to question my own self-worth.

My usually strong exterior crumbled, and the next thing I knew I was in tears. The unfairness of the situation had overcome me completely and had climaxed due to months of the 'office politics' that had worn me down. It was at this time that I realised I was creeping towards the territory commonly referred to as the 'glass ceiling' — a metaphor used, according the U.S. Department of Labor, to describe 'the unseen, yet unbreakable barrier that keeps minorities and women from rising to the upper rungs of the corporate ladder, regardless of their qualifications or achievements'. As already mentioned,

I decided I couldn't put up with the situation and needed to resign.

For further information on Linda Ray and her SCARE model, go to neurocapability.com.au. Once there, you can also check out her training programs for individuals, including her Neuroscience of Leadership program and the Advanced Diploma of Neuroscience of Leadership.

As a final activity for this chapter, order each of the five SCARE factors — Significance, Certainty, Autonomy, Relatedness and Equity — in terms of how important they are to you (most important to least important).

SCARE Domain	1 = Most Important / 5 = Least Important
Significance	
Certainty	
Autonomy	
Relatedness	
Equity	

Think about how your ordering of these factors affects your leadership style. Do you have some blind spots? Are you focusing on providing rewards in particular areas while ignoring threats in others? Try to ensure you're aware of all five SCARE factors, and the work you need to do in all of them.

For now, just focus on you. I provide some ideas to help you think about how your staff might order them in the following chapter.

Janine Allis and Boost Juice

The story of Janine Allis, founder of Boost Juice and now part owner of Retail Zoo, is incredibly inspirational. Boost Juice is a brand synonymous with healthy living in Australia, and Janine brings the VACAS leadership styles outlined in chapter 2 to life throughout her journey.

Founded in 2000, Boost Juice opened their first store in Adelaide, Australia. Janine (along with her business partner and husband, Jeff) quickly decided to implement a franchise model, and Boost Juice has since grown to 580 stores in 12 regions across the world. Janine and Jeff went on to purchase more businesses under their umbrella company Retail Zoo. In 2010, they sold 70 per cent of Retail Zoo for $70 million, with the company reporting revenue of more than $220 million in 2022–23.

While Jeff and Janine started Boost Juice together, Janine was always in the leadership seat. Janine had a vision that 'every customer will leave a Boost Juice store feeling just that little bit better', and her philosophy is simply 'love life' – an attitude she brings to every facet of her life. Janine lived and breathed this approach even through the first three years of trials and tribulations at the start of the business – before all her hard work started to pay off and then catapulted her into success.

Janine has won many awards, including the following:

- Franchise Hall of Fame Inductee, MYOB FCA Excellence in Franchising Awards (2015)
- Excellence in Women's Leadership: Victoria, The Australian Business Awards (2015)
- Business Award, InStyle and Audi Women of Style Awards (2015)
- Australian Export Heroes Award, Export Council of Australia (2012)
- International Franchise Award, Franchise Council of Australia (2010)
- Australian Business Woman of the Year, Telstra (2004)

Applying the VACAS model to Janine Allis

I developed my VACAS model from the lessons (sometimes conscious, sometimes accidental) I learnt from good and bad bosses. The model developed over time through constant critique and practice, as I turned it into the polished and practical methodology it is today. In a similar way, the leaders you have worked with – along with well-known leaders of today and yesterday – have most likely moulded you into the leader you will become tomorrow. Janine argues, 'People teach you how to be a boss. The first thing I learned was that when someone was my leader, what did I like about their management, or not like?'

So how does Janine's leadership stack up when the VACAS model is applied to it?

Visionary

Janine has often spoken about the importance of a leader who clearly sees the company vision and, just as importantly, can clearly communicate this vision. According to Janine, 'It's all very well having great ideas, but if you can't articulate them and get people on the same journey as you, then you'll go nowhere.' Furthermore, an employee's belief in the journey gives a sense of belonging and purpose, which is a critical part to getting your staff to stick around.

Authenticity

Janine calls a spade a spade. Her approach to everything she does and says is authentic, giving you a very real sense of who she is and where you would stand if you had the pleasure in working closely with her. Her authenticity is apparent throughout her well-known story of starting the Boost Juice brand from her kitchen at home. It's there when she admits to being 'flawed' and feeling like she had got it all wrong at times – like sending her kids to school in the wrong uniform. And it's there when she outlines her commonsense approach of paving her own way to business dominance, even while confessing she had little business knowledge when she started. Authenticity is definitely not about getting it right all the time; however, owning your mistakes and learning from them, coupled with perseverance, holds you in great stead for success.

Coaching

Coaching can come from anyone. In Janine's case, her husband, Jeff, was her biggest cheerleader in the early days of establishing Boost Juice. Janine highlights that Jeff 'had more faith in me in those early days than I had in myself'. Wherever the coaching comes from, a true coach ensures each staff member is in the centre of their role and offers the level of support that is required in that moment.

Authoritative

Again, while I don't condone the Authoritative leadership style in everyday dealings with staff (as emphasised in chapter 2), Janine is on the mark when she states, 'If you are a leader, be a strong, confident leader that can make decisions and follow through'. That 'follow through' – doing what you say you are going to do – gives people confidence in your ability to actually lead! And that confidence in those decisions you have made also enables Visionary leadership, which means the direction you want to take your business in actually crystallises.

Servant

As outlined in chapter 2, Servant leadership is all about removing hurdles for your people, and then getting out of the way and letting them flourish. Janine also incorporates this into her leadership, and a digital manager 'gun' she hired to work for her is an example of this. Describing her role when he started, Janine told him it was her job to 'clear the freeway for him' – meaning she was there to remove hurdles and give him all the runway he needed to succeed in the job he had been hired to do.

Bringing in mindset

While all VACAS leadership styles are clearly evident in Janine's journey, what is also clearly valuable for this phenomenal woman is a healthy mindset. Having discovered the power of attraction through a recommended book, Janine recognised the importance of controlling her thoughts and building up the muscle in her mind to effectively swap out negative thoughts to positive ones, believing that the 'power of how you think really dictates your happiness'.

Top Tips
Leading Yourself

Clearly define your values:

- *What's happening:* When you don't have clearly defined values, staying in control of your environment and path is difficult. Misalignments between yourself and your workplace can occur, which makes your day-to-day life more challenging than it really needs to be. However, when you clearly define these values and match them to your workplace, this alignment provides cohesion that sets you up for success.

- *How to control it:* Work through the values activity in chapter 1 to uncover your own beacons. Once you have these, compare them to the values of your workplace and be brutally honest about the alignment to your own. If you uncover a misalignment, do something about it. Find a new workplace or, if you own your business, start the journey to recreating your own culture using these beacons as your guiding light, for they are the soul and backbone of a successful workplace.

Control your environment:

- *What's happening:* When juggling so many tasks that it causes you constant stress, cortisol is released. Cortisol helps you to determine the source of stress and then decide how to respond. Too much cortisol being released, however, results in fatigue and irritability. The continued presence of cortisol in your bloodstream negatively affects your emotional stability, and eventually your long-term health.

- *How to control it:* Get ideas and tasks out of your head and on to paper or your device – this immediately frees up space in your prefrontal cortex. Focus on one task at a time. The prefrontal cortex finds holding any more than four ideas at a given time difficult. This reduces to two ideas if a decision is to be made, and just one idea if a task is to be completed. Turn off all external distractions – including email alerts and other notifications. Say 'no' and block out time in your calendar for thinking, planning, even reading books to help keep your mind in check. Find something really funny to laugh at as much as you can. Laughter releases more oxygen to the brain, and more oxygen means your brain is better fuelled (remember the brain uses 20 per cent of all the body's oxygen). Laughter also causes endorphins to surge, which are the body's natural painkillers.

Identify your VACAS and SCARE strengths and weaknesses:

- *What's happening:* Naturally, you will be higher in one or two of the VACAS leadership styles or SCARE domains. Play to those strengths, but make sure to identify the lower domains too. It is important to have these balanced to ensure you are setting yourself – and your team – up for success.

- *How to control it:* Regularly complete the VACAS inventory (refer to chapter 2) and work on developing any weaknesses with additional research and study. Also complete the SCARE activity at the end of chapter 4 to be self-aware of your higher domains, and which factors may be creating threats (or rewards) for your staff.

PART II

>>

LEADING YOUR PEOPLE

A really big focus for me is my team's growth, and I love nothing more than watching them succeed and get that confidence in themselves — it's my favourite part of the job. All the coaching and development models I cover in this part are what enable me to encourage such growth in quite a methodical way. For women, our world often centres on our biggest job of all — being mums. We nurture, we encourage and we have bucket loads of empathy for our kids (well, most of the time). All this often naturally translates across to our staff. Studies show this is why women tend to hold on to staff longer than men. Interestingly, according to a Personal Finance Club 2022 report that looked at women-led companies versus men-led companies, over the past 10 years, the women-led companies have out-performed the others. The difference in returns was 384 per cent from companies with female CEOs versus 261 per cent from companies with male CEOs. Coincidence? I think not!

I once had an employee who was achieving only a few hundred dollars a day in sales, when the target was $1200. When she came to me, she was so lacking in confidence from how she was treated in her previous place of work. Through consistent coaching, encouragement and development, she's now one of my top sellers, regularly achieving between $1200 and $1400 a day, and sometimes even more than that. Seeing her grow and gain confidence has been an awesome experience for me as her leader. I have countless staff who have similar stories to this with their development and growth — one of my clinic managers being the most recent. I drip-fed her the responsibilities of the role so she could really grow into it and flourish. As I said, seeing your staff go from strength to strength and watching them succeed at their own goals is a really fun part of the job.

We have such a great responsibility when we're leading a team of people, and I do wonder how much some people think about this prior to taking the responsibility on. I wonder if they consider the impact they might have — either good or bad. I can still remember the names of the school teachers who made an impact on me — good and bad. And the same is true of the leaders I've had.

A good teacher is worth so much to our kids, and so too is a good leader to adults. As a leader, you have the power to inflict serious dread in people, or inspire serious inspiration and joy — and, of course, everything in-between. When experiencing a bad line manager, 82 per cent of people will consider leaving a business (according to a 2022 survey from GoodHire), while 57 per cent actually do leave (highlighted in DDI's 2019 Frontline Leader Project). These are massive numbers and a big unnecessary cost. Don't let this happen to you! You're in charge of rounding out your own leadership development and building a great culture. It starts and stops at the top.

As a leader, you have a responsibility to your people to create environments for them to grow into the best they can be. You are responsible for their welfare at work. If you feel you have gaps in your leadership skillset, plug those gaps as quickly as you can, because you owe this to your people.

On many occasions, I have seen people promoted because they were excellent at their roles, only to move into management and come unstuck because they do not have the necessary skills to lead a team. Leadership is a learned skillset and one that should be continuously developed.

What's interesting is that people rarely tell you when entering your leadership career that having courage and perseverance might be two of the most valuable attributes you can have. It takes courage to go into bat for your team against your boss, or your boss's boss. It takes courage to present a new project in front of the executive or senior leadership team. It takes courage and perseverance to lead when you are in the middle of a pandemic (which we've all had to do in recent years). It takes courage and perseverance to stay the course on a strategy in the face of overwhelming pressure to deviate. We need courage and perseverance in so many areas in the daily life of a leader, especially a female leader. In the chapters in this part, I provide an overview of recruitment and how you can formulate a high-performing team. I look again at SCARE (from chapter 4) but through the lens of a manager, rather than as an individual. Understanding SCARE in this context provides further depth and understanding, and supports you to maintain the cohesive, high-performing culture following the creation of your team through optimised productivity. I also go through several frameworks relevant to increasing accountability, developing your staff and, finally, succession planning to sustain the team you have created.

As you move through this part, remembering a simple acronym framework is useful: HPPS. This stands for Happier, Productive, Profitable and Sustainable, and HPPS has always lined my thoughts when creating and developing my teams. Many studies support the idea that happier staff are more productive. And if they are more productive, they are likely to be more profitable. If these three aspects are achieved, you are more likely to have sustainability in your team and business, meaning you can focus on the things that you should be focusing on.

CHAPTER 5

Recruiting staff and developing high performance

A good team curation will take time. When I bought my business and inherited the original team, it took me approximately 18 months.

Putting in the required time and effort is well worth it, because good people attract good people. Once you are known for a great culture, good people will find you. Top performers who know your existing top performers will approach you and will be drawn to working in your team as if by a magnetic force.

At a time when finding staff is getting increasingly difficult and the pendulum has swung to the side of the employee, maintaining your culture must become one of the most important things you can do. You can't control a lot of aspects in business (which you no doubt know all too well following COVID and/or recent natural disasters), but you can control your culture, and this is done by living and breathing the strong set of people-centric values you put in place. Back in chapter 1, I outline the values I needed to align in my business in order for it to succeed (these being the fundamentals of being upbeat, and having a sense of fun, happiness, trust, security and focus). Your recruitment strategy must also align to your values to ensure you are creating the type of culture you want, with the type of people you want.

Focusing on culture

Without identifying your values, culture will still exist in your team or business, but you may find it is not the culture you want. It could also be one that controls you rather than you controlling it. The CEO of a company I once worked for would often repeat the quote 'Culture eats strategy for breakfast' — a quote made famous by management consultant and writer Peter Drucker. The basic idea behind this is that, no matter how well-designed your strategic plan is, it will fall flat unless your team shares the appropriate culture to carry out the strategy. But I have always disagreed with the sentiment behind this statement, and still do.

Sure, culture can eat strategy for breakfast, but given that the values for the business should be incorporated at the highest level when developing your strategic intent (i.e. what you as a business are trying to achieve) — which culture should then cascade from — if culture is eating strategy for breakfast, aren't you (as the leader at the top), failing in living, inspiring and influencing the people-centric values of your business? Consequently, your highest level of strategy — your strategic intent — which of course includes your values, has failed and yes, your culture has thus eaten your strategy for breakfast.

However, if the leader is succeeding in achieving their overall strategic intent — which again, 'should' include the values the leader aspires to have in their organisation — they would therefore have value alignment from their collective staff on what they are trying to do and how they go about doing it, as not only would they be living and breathing these values, but they would be attracting and inspiring people who share these values too. In this case, they would have contributed to achieving the culture they want, which has been built from the company's highest level of strategy. And so, I would argue, it is your 'strategy that eats culture for breakfast'.

A well-known petrol company in New Zealand is Z Energy. (The former Shell operations were sold and rebranded as Z Energy when Shell left the NZ fuel distribution business in 2010.) The company is a perfect example of a major corporation that rediscovered and redefined themselves with a brand-new set of people-centric values. Following their rebranding, their new CEO devised a flawless strategy. He lived and breathed their defined values, and eventually so did his people. Over the next four years, Z Energy managed to build their business to four times the value it had been purchased for. (For more on Z Energy, see the case study at the end of part III.)

However, in saying all that, it is important to understand that culture is fluid. It is forever changing based on what is going on in your team members' lives and what is going on in the market. Culture can change almost in an instant, so you need to be constantly hands-on when managing it. And when you do get it to that sweet spot where everything is optimised, the culture then needs to be vigorously protected — above all else. The SCARE model (refer to chapter 4) is your vehicle to do just that.

Developing your recruitment strategy

When I was in the middle management part of my career, I had a manager who taught me the value of a good recruitment strategy. He was so thorough with the entire process — from not just reading but fully analysing the resume, to working through the attributes a person must have that would require them to be successful in the role. We even went as far as doing a weighted calculation against those required attributes, which would spit out a quantitative result and give each prospective employee a percentage score on suitability in our team and in the role.

Obviously, many psychometric testing platforms are available to employers these days, and we did all that kind of testing also; however, I have always found completing this thorough but simple weighted process worked best for creating the cohesive and high-performing team we all strive for as leaders.

When you really sit down and think about what is important to you personally as the manager leading a group of people, and then really think about what attributes are important for the prospective employees to possess in order to perform in the role in question, you actually sum up exactly what you are looking for — in the resume, in the interview, in the psychometric testing, and even in their first 90 days.

Knowing these attributes makes it easy within those first 90 days to identify that if things are going wrong and, if so, where exactly they're going wrong. Sometimes, for example, a person's interview behaviour is not consistent with their actual behaviour once in the job.

Speaking of the first 90 days, the same manager who taught me recruitment strategy also bought me the book *The First 90 Days* by leadership and organisational change expert Michael Watkins (originally published in 2006). This book was instrumental in my success early in my leadership career, because it helps you to plan, gain credibility through small and quick wins, and uncover your blind spots to ensure your plan succeeds.

At the time of learning this recruitment strategy, I wrote down the attributes required for a role we were looking to fill. Interestingly, no matter what team I've since led or what role I was recruiting for, the same attributes have applied. These attributes are as follows:

- Work under pressure (links to the security and focus values).

- Attention to detail (links to focus value).

- Rapport building (links to fun, security and trust values).

- Confident communicator (links to security and trust values).

- Punctual (links to trust and security values).

- Professional image (links to focus value) and tidy appearance, both written and in person.

- Self-motivator (links to focus, trust and security values).

Importantly, I asked applicants to prove the final attribute in the preceding list using something they did outside of work. For example, I interviewed one girl who had a cake-baking business on the side. It was her hobby but she made a little bit of extra cash from doing something she was passionate about, and I respected that. Another of my prospective employees was a leader at the Christian camp he attended every year. I also had two staff members who had put themselves through an MBA — I respected that also. Hanging with friends on the weekend, however, is not necessarily something I would rate highly here!

Using a weighted decision matrix

As mentioned, a weighted decision matrix can help you quantify your best applicant. The weighting you attach to each attribute reflects what you believe is the most versus the least important — just make sure the total figure adds up to 100 per cent. (See table 5.1 for an example of how these weightings can be distributed.)

You then give each prospective employee a score out of 10 for each of the attributes. The score is multiplied by the weighting, and added to the other attributes to give you a weighted decision score. (The first column in table 5.1 shows this multiplication for Jonathan, one of the applicants.)

Table 5.1 A weighted decision matrix example

Attribute	Weighting	Jonathan	Mark	Liz
Work under pressure	25%	8 (× 25% = 2)	4	8
Attention to detail	15%	7 (× 15% = 1.05)	4	6
Rapport building	15%	4 (× 15% = 0.6)	8	7
Confident communicator	18%	6 (× 18% = 1.08)	8	7
Professional image	7%	9 (× 7% = 0.63)	5	3
Punctual	10%	4 (× 10% = 0.4)	6	7
Self-motivator	10%	8 (× 10% = 0.8)	5	7
Totals	100%	6.56	5.69	6.82

Based on the example shown in table 5.1, you can see that Liz came in with the best score, and is who will get the job!

Interviewing

When you're forming your squad of staff and are on your way to building your dream team, it is important that these people get a warm welcome right from the get-go. My interview technique is not one of a clinical nature and could sometimes be construed as unorthodox. It is relaxed, welcoming and warm. You need to start how you intend to continue.

Interviews by their very nature can be intimidating. This means the prospective employee is already in a threat state, which will naturally limit their ability to show who they really are — because, as already covered, they don't have the oxygen where it needs to be in their prefrontal cortex to think as freely as they would otherwise. My job in that room, therefore, is to make the person feel as comfortable as I can as quickly as I can. I don't sit on the opposite side of the desk, for example, because this puts a barrier up between us. I sit next to them on the same side of the desk if I have to interview in the office. However, if it is possible to do so, I like to interview at a cafe or even a pub over a beer and talk to the person like I have known them for years.

I then see them visibly relax after about 5 or 10 minutes — after we've chatted about their drive in, compared morning rushing around routines with kids, or just the weather. I use anything I can to get them talking about themselves and to get them comfortable. Often, if they have put something in their resume under hobbies and interests, I look for a common thread that we can relate over. I was into horses in my younger years, so if they were into that too we could spend considerable time talking horses!

Once I start to see them visibly relax, I then start to ask any of my specific 'interview questions', albeit still in a conversational way. Try this technique yourself. You'll likely get responses that are much more authentic when you have built up relatability and rapport.

As mentioned in the previous section, I also like to ask interviewees for an example from their lives outside work that shows they are self-motivated. To discuss this further, I would get them talking about something I've picked out of their CV that I think determines them as a self-motivator — for example, completing an MBA. Getting them talking about that aspect of their CV raises their confidence in the interview. This means I can see exactly how they would be after they have gained confidence in the new role. If they speak with courage of conviction and are engaging, I know they are going to be excellent after they are trained in the new role.

As mentioned, once you are known for a great culture, good people will find you. You may be able to streamline your recruitment process or employ managers to recruit on your behalf. In this situation, still ensure you always remain involved in the recruitment process to a certain degree. You want to crosscheck yourself that the value alignment is present with every new employee to maintain the culture you have worked so hard to get!

Onboarding

Once I'd selected a new team member, and while I was in the initial 18 months of building my team, each new member would receive a gift pack on arrival and a handwritten card welcoming them to the team. On this card, each of the staff had written their own person note.

Oxytocin (the relatability hormone) was being released in abundance in this early stage, as the staff member was made to feel connected to the team very quickly through the handwritten card. I included in the gift pack a copy of *Mind Power into the 21st Century* (discussed in chapter 1). And I added a candle and a few skincare products from the range in our clinic. The gift and card were, of course, a nice touch, but the strength of this onboarding strategy lay in the book.

Having all new team members read this book meant that everyone was on the same page with how they could control their thoughts — so important for everyone, and sometimes even more so for women. This also helped ensure we were all manifesting and aligning towards the same goal. This has also been a vital part of our success.

⏱ PRODUCTIVITY TIP

When someone is new in a job, providing clarity of social norms and being very clear on what the business requires is important to ensure the team remains cohesive and high performing.

Ensuring your team remains cohesive and all focused on the same goals also requires strict and swift action to be taken if you spot any low performers or if any toxicity in people is brewing. You need to be willing and prepared to make an example out of people should the need arise.

As an example, a woman recently started with us. On paper she was excellent, but it only took about three weeks before we started to see some toxic behaviour creep in. Because we have built a culture on no drama, happiness, fun and trust, she stood out very quickly in all the wrong ways. I acted swiftly by working through our formal HR process and having the required discussions with her. However, she didn't like this, and resigned. I also made a point of talking to two of the other girls who had gotten tangled into some of the toxic behaviour. I sat them down and said what I needed to say to make them clear on what was acceptable and what was not in terms of our behaviours. I did this easily by objectively comparing the unacceptable behaviours to our strong set of values. This took the issue away from any person in particular, which therefore took out any emotion. With a staff of 10 to 13 women in a small business, I am proud to say we do not have any of the usual unkind behaviours that can sometimes emerge. And this is because both my managers and I are aligned with what we will put up with and what we will not. Therefore, culturally, the whole team is very clear also, because the same messages come through from all of us, whether someone is a leader in the business or not.

We also run through an onboarding checklist. This is split over two phases of time, with the time lines being determined by the manager. In phase one, we focus more on the theory of the role and run through the required online modules, including treatment protocols and health and safety requirements. In phase two, we cover the intricacies of the booking system and the more practical elements of the role. This ensures we uncover every aspect, at the right time, to enable a smooth entry into the business. We use a staged approach to ensure we are not overwhelming the new starter.

Another important aspect is our use of a buddy system, with the 'buddy' typically being our trainer, who ensures the new employee's skills are aligned to the rest of the group. The new starter shadows the trainer for their first few days and the trainer also acts as a friend and confidant to the employee to allow them to settle in happier and quicker.

If I'm onboarding a new manager, we discuss the ideas and processes outlined in *The First 90 Days* by Michael

Watkins (mentioned earlier in this chapter), and I ask the new manager to produce their own 90-day plan.

Using SCARE

I cover the SCARE model in detail in chapter 4. In this section, I provide some further examples of how I have used the concepts to help maintain the reward state with my teams to increase productivity in the team environment.

Significance

I provide very clear promotion triggers for my workforce. This means, when a staff member has developed their required skillset and can display consistent sales/net promoter score (NPS) target results, they know they will be rewarded with a promotion—whether that's from Junior to Middle, or Middle to Senior level. There is no ambiguity on this. The staff are always growing their skillset and working towards their next skillset or promotion.

> ### ⏱ PRODUCTIVITY TIP
>
> Ensuring staff are clear on targets – and rewarding them consistently when they achieve them – keeps your team in the reward state and feeds into their intrinsic need for high levels of Significance among their peers. This breeds loyalty and productivity.

In my current Laser Clinics Australia business, we have a Facebook messenger group as our main means of communication. When I was in the corporate world, this type of communication would have been via group emails or, of course, phone and text. Whatever platform you use to keep all staff in the loop, the main principles remain. When we have had a particularly good day of sales or a staff member is signed off on a new level of accountability, I use the group chat to call out whoever needs congratulating—particularly any new starters. Often the team will all then chime in to do the same. This increases the receiver's Significance reward circuitry, and I time and again see the same positive patterns of behaviour and strong results occur in the following days and weeks. As this occurs, their confidence grows until their higher performance simply becomes the norm. This consistent positive feedback loop perpetuates the supportive culture that cultivates outstanding results.

Certainty

In addition to providing clear promotion triggers, I also give staff clarity in where the business or department is going in terms of growth. This links in the requirements of Visionary leadership, and increases the Certainty reward state for staff. By providing them a 'now' and 'future' organisational chart, for example, they have certainty that their jobs are safe and, better than that, they have clear progression possibilities in the business or department that they can grow into.

 **PRODUCTIVITY TIP**

Making sure you are mapping out staff members' progression while also providing the relevant skill development provides the Certainty reward circuitry required for high productivity.

Being inauthentic and failing to provide consistent parameters to work within can produce a Certainty threat status. Even something as simple as stating what a meeting is about and how long it will run for can help bring team members back over to the Certainty reward state.

Autonomy

Regular weekly or fortnightly one-to-ones are a great framework to work within to ensure all staff are working towards the same long-term goals. You can use quarterly KPIs and your established strategy as the guiding lights to direct you. Holding these meetings consistently — and not letting them slip as other needs take priority — helps to keep the Certainty needs of staff met. And then ensuring these meetings are collaborative helps to meet their Autonomy needs.

For example, in the meeting you and your staff member can work together to create action lists for the following period. When creating these lists, questions such as 'Here are two options that could work. Which would you prefer?' are more effective than saying something like, 'Here is what you have to do now' for the Autonomy reward circuitry. As mentioned earlier, you can clearly see this in action with kids. If I tell my child to wear a particular t-shirt', he will almost always refuse. But if I give him two options to pick from, he will always choose one of them. Kids are the easiest of humans to try all applied neuroscience out on because they wear their hearts on their sleeves — their emotional circuitry is still maturing and they're not yet able to fully rationalise. So if they don't like what you're putting down, you'll know about it!

Allowing your team member to determine the one-to-one action activities they commit to means they are exerting their own control. This increases the perception of Autonomy and increases the reward circuitry. As their leader and manager, you can guide them to ensure they are meeting appropriate targets aligned with company objectives; however, they are effectively producing their own lists for which they are accountable each week.

Allowing staff to manage their own working hours or providing options of working from home are further examples of how the Autonomy reward state can be achieved and prove beneficial for all, if done within agreed parameters.

Relatedness

In one of my leadership roles, my team and I collaboratively created a strategy called 20/20/20. This stood for $20 000 000 in revenue for our department, growing to 20 people in the team, by the year 2020. We even had our own logo created. It was such an engaging strategy that we had several people from other departments saying they wanted to join our team.

At one of the quarterly offsites we had, I produced a gift pack for each of the team members. In this gift pack was a key ring with 20/20/20 on it. All these years later, some of the team, including me, still have that keyring due to the sense of connection and belonging — that is, our Relatedness to each other — being so strong within that team.

You can use similar strategies to build a sense of connection and Relatedness in your team. Other options for increasing the rewards for Relatedness include ensuring a buddy system or providing a mentor at work is central to your workplace engagement. Getting to know your colleagues personally through Authentic leadership also releases oxytocin and helps collaboration.

Equity

An example of something so simple that ensures a sense of Equity and fairness across our team is discussing roster changes with everyone to ensure their buy-in, rather than just handing changes out with little regard for aspects such as set day care days and other things people often have to juggle outside work.

When I originally prepared the roster in my business after I had built the core team, I threw the roster over to the staff so they could work together to create their ideal roster. Given our business runs seven days a week, this was no small task. The staff did an exemplary job and, since then, we have had very few problems. While it can be challenging at times to make pieces of the puzzle fit, we continue to ensure it is done in such a way that is fair and reasonable — in other words, in a way that increases the Equity reward. This process is now so culturally engrained that everyone supports each other.

Let's look at the SCARE factors once more. This time order each of the five SCARE factors — Significance, Certainty, Autonomy, Relatedness and Equity — in terms of how important you think they are to your staff (most important to least important).

SCARE Domain	1 = Most Important / 5 = Least Important
Significance	
Certainty	
Autonomy	
Relatedness	
Equity	

Now compare the most important SCARE factors for your staff with the ones you ranked as most important at the end of part I. Are they the same? Or do you have different priorities? Again, do you have any blind spots or areas that need more attention? Work collaboratively with your team to work out their needs and any areas you need to shift from a threat to a reward state.

CHAPTER 6
Development and coaching models

In the previous chapter, I cover forming your squad of staff and communicating with them clearly to help ensure their SCARE needs are met, and they stay in a reward state to improve productivity. But your work with your staff doesn't stop there! You have to keep up your coaching, and continue to develop your staff.

In this chapter, I take you through some common coaching and development models, providing an overview of their main areas of focus and how you can apply this to your team. I also cover that important — but sometimes overlooked — area of succession planning. Again, if any model particularly grabs you, you can use the resources provided to research it further and dive more deeply into its applications.

GROW model

The GROW model was developed by leadership development expert Sir John Whitmore, and outlined in his 2009 book *Coaching for Performance* (now in its fifth edition). Using this model helps you to orientate conversations with your team (or individual staff members) efficiently and effectively, rather than them turning into a frustrating merry-go-round. It also allows you to quickly take advantage of any coaching moments that occur throughout your day. Each day can bring so many coaching moments but sometimes we are so busy that we miss the opportunity to provide these important lessons. The GROW model can help you be effective in just a two-minute conversation so it is certainly a worthwhile model to explore and practise.

The GROW acronym stands for:

- *Goal:* Here you are simply trying to ascertain what the employee you're talking with wants. For example, if an employee who has come to you with an issue is simply wanting to vent, or needs a specific outcome.

- *Reality:* This part is about understanding the situation, and getting the employee to fill you in on what they know. At this stage as the leader, asking open and leading questions is important to help you understand the full picture.

- *Options:* This stage is about working through with the employee the options they have to solve their plight. Importantly, the employee needs to work through this mostly themselves — with your guidance only — to ensure the lesson is engrained.

- *Wrap up:* This stage is simply that — a wrap up of the conversation and what has been agreed to. Accountability is set on who will do what, and a follow-up is scheduled if required.

Most staff will come to you and jump straight to spilling the details required in the Reality phase. As leader, it is your job to redirect them to first outline the Goal of the conversation, and so determine their desired outcome. Once this is done, you can go further down the rabbit hole of the Reality stage and draw out all the information required before working through the Options available to them, and finally Wrapping up the conversation.

Accountability/competency matrix

The accountability/competency matrix simply provides a way of mapping your staff on a graph to know where they sit in terms of the accountability given to them in a role and their competence to do that role. You can use this exercise when you have staff who want to progress and continue to learn and develop their careers (and these are employees you want to keep). I recommend doing this exercise at least quarterly.

Figure 6.1 (overleaf) provides an example of how this matrix might play out. Say you have an employee who is on low accountability but with high competency — in the provided figure, this is Bob. If you're not doing anything to progress Bob, whether that be through additional training or promotions, you can expect to lose him sometime soon. Conversely, say you have an employee who has been given lots of accountability but has low competency to achieve what is being expected of them. This is Mary on the provided matrix. You've effectively thrown Mary in the deep end without checking whether she can swim and with no support, and you can also expect to lose her. Or worse, you knock Mary's confidence so badly that she has self-esteem issues for years to come, affecting her future work prospects. Or even worse still, Mary was a manager when you gave all this accountability, and her lack of leadership competence negatively affected the employees under her. You can see why some workplaces get into such bad shape.

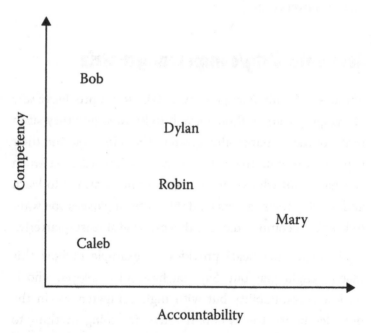

Figure 6.1 An accountability/competency matrix example

Instead of competency and accountability being unbalanced in this way, you want both aspects to be about even for all your staff members. Based on this, you can see that Caleb is in about the right position for this stage in his career, with his lower competency reflected in his lower accountability. The same is also true for Dylan and Robin, where their increased competency is again reflected in their increased accountability.

When I started one of my leadership roles, I inherited the manager already in place. Unfortunately, the accountability of the role she had been asked to do outweighed her competence at the time. Consequently, she was consumed and overwhelmed by her responsibilities, and perhaps destined for failure in that role. By the time I got there, a culture of eggshells and intimidation was already engrained due to her being so on edge all the time and in a constant state of overwhelm. As her leader, all I could do was manage the situation as best I could, and provide every possible leadership training and coaching opportunity for this manager. Despite this, and perhaps inevitably, one day she spontaneously combusted. The constant pressure of the role was simply too much for her and, while I am sure she did not mean to create such a tense environment and subsequent culture, this unfortunately happened because of her lack of ability to fulfil the leadership component of the role. Her people did not trust or respect her, and coming back from that is very hard — not impossible, but it is difficult, especially without accepting or taking accountability of your own failings and shortcomings. Authenticity and accountability are vital for leaders in any situation but especially when we make mistakes. Making mistakes is inevitable but owning them outright and being sincere in your apologies is the key to coming back and winning trust and respect again.

Severe warning signs popped up in the lead-up to the spontaneous combustion event. One in particular occurred when we were doing a one-to-one with one of the senior employees. The tension in that room was palpable. The manager was convinced of the employee's lack of ability, yet this employee had come to us full of promise and with many excellent references to boot. I also had the strong instinct this employee was a gem — an absolute keeper — so, needless to say, I had a bit of cognitive dissonance present. I was on edge myself in that room because I did not want to undermine the manager, especially because I was still very new in my role. I also wanted to be seen as supporting my manager who, up until this point, had kept the business afloat single-handedly and had proven herself to be operationally excellent — however, as we've learnt, leadership is about much more than being operationally excellent.

It was quickly coming apparent during this one-to-one meeting that the problem was the manager, not the employee. The catalyst was seeing the employee's spirit literally break in front of my very eyes. She had been so worn down by this manager over the short time of her employ and was clearly distraught at the unfairness of the situation, but she could not articulate her way through the haze of gaslighting. I had been in her position once earlier in my career with 'Rick' (refer to chapter 4) so, luckily for her, I did see through it.

I ended the meeting at that point and sent the manager out. I sat with the employee, leant her a much needed ear, and gave her a hug. And then I waited for the manager's inevitable spontaneous combustion event, knowing it would come soon. Unfortunately, I could see all the support and coaching I was giving this manager were having no effect. It was all coming too late, and she was in a downward spiral. With the manager's departure, I could start doing something about righting her wrongs.

Sometimes as a leader you may have done all you can with a particular member of staff to coach them and provide them every opportunity to lift their competencies and succeed and grow, but you find it is still simply not working. In cases like these, don't be afraid to cut ties and start over. It can be the best, and most cost-effective, solution to the situation. You are both either swimming in the current together or you are not, and it's best to learn or admit that sooner rather than later.

After the manager left the business, I took over her role myself to learn everything there was to learn about managing the business. By the time I hired the person who was to become the next manager, I had turned over every stone there was to turn. I also had a genuine appreciation for the enormity of the role. Being a seven-day-a-week business, if this management role was not properly understood — and properly supported — burnout wasn't just a risk, it was an eventuality.

The new manager was inexperienced in leadership and we were quite different in terms of personality, but she held the exact same values, ethics and integrity that I did. Together, using the set of values we lived and breathed, we hired a bunch of staff who were well suited to us, and to the business. This bred team cohesion, psychological safety and, ultimately, high performance.

Seeing so clearly the issues surrounding the first manager, I was very careful not to overwhelm the new one. I drip-fed her each of the responsibilities of the role when I believed she could handle it. I started simply with training and upskilling the team. When she was showing signs of competency in her existing responsibilities, I gave her more. Ensuring she was challenged but not overwhelmed was a constant balancing act. I also diluted the role slightly by surrounding her with a very strong leadership team. In time, we hired a trainer, who took care of the training needs of the staff, along with an assistant manager who worked on the manager's days off. This meant the manager was not pulled into any issues or tasks on her days off and could actually enjoy them, and thus mitigating the risk of burnout. This also meant that if the manager had annual leave, the place didn't fall apart — at least two people at any time could step in and do her role while she was gone.

The entire situation with my manager was orchestrated using the SCARE model and, again, the Goldilocks principle of getting the balance between accountability and competency 'just right'. Ultimately, this helped to ensure productivity remained consistently high.

In the following section, I outline some ways you can tweak your competencies versus accountability expectations.

80 per cent accomplishment rule

Often, your staff member may not have the full matured skillset to be able to do a task that has been allocated to them as well as if you did it yourself. In this case, you might like to apply the 80 per cent rule. The crux of the 80 per cent rule is, when assigning a new task to the employee, you don't need to be certain they will be fully competent in the task right from the start, as long as you continue to provide coaching following the completion of the task.

PRODUCTIVITY TIP

If a staff member produces a result on a new task that is around 80 per cent of what you would have done yourself, this is an excellent result – so tell them so! Over time, that employee will build up their competency until they can achieve 100 per cent. In the meantime, this 80 per cent rule can keep any unjustified frustration at bay.

You can tweak this rule according to the task and the employee you're allocating it to. Depending on the level of the employee, for example, an 80 per cent expectation can sometimes drop to 50 per cent.

3:1 ratio rule

When considering competencies versus accountability, I never focus solely on a negative performance issue with a staff member that is hindering their progress or growth. Instead, I apply the 3:1 ratio rule, with the negative aspect the '1' in the 3:1 ratio. Using the ratio means I also focus on three attributes or skills that the staff member naturally gravitates towards and is good at already — in other words, the '3' in my 3:1 ratio. We can then focus on making those three even better.

As an example, one of my managers needed development in performing administrative duties. However, she was an excellent trainer and therapist, which were the other main requirements of her role. With clients, she showed empathy and kindness, yet with a strength that gave anyone in her aura confidence in her advice for them. She was cool as a cucumber under pressure and when she was being pulled in every which way — with phones going, clients coming and going, and staff coming to her with questions — she remained in control in every situation. Eventually, these skills meant she progressed through into the manager role. In this role, administration was an important task and so her weaknesses in this area would hinder her ability to fulfil the role. I therefore gave her the space and support needed so she could progress in this one development issue she needed to overcome.

Coming back to the 3:1 ratio rule, the three positive attributes or skills I supported her on improving were her (already pretty excellent) skills in customer experience, team leadership and daily structure. The one attribute or skill we needed to work on was administration.

Succession planning

Once you hit a senior level where you have managers reporting to you, having just one team leader or manager in your team or business isn't enough. Instead, you should aim to have at least one to two other staff members who, at any point, could step into the manager's role — or at least be able to perform a reasonable amount of their operational duties. Otherwise, not only will things fall over when they aren't there, but you will also always be pulled back into a role that is not yours just to keep the place running, pulling your focus from the strategic growth of the business and other important matters. In addition, if you are running a seven-days-a-week business, surrounding your manager with a leadership team is worthwhile, because this helps to shoulder the responsibility across the days — again, avoiding the eventual risk of burnout.

Recently I had one of my assistant managers leave the business. Because we were able to replace them in this role with one of our senior employees, we experienced very little disruption to the day-to-day running of the business and were able to maintain our high performance.

In many of my corporate leadership positions, I had a clear 2IC (second in command) who I kept close. This person was highly involved in the strategy of the department and business, and was often involved in staff one-to-ones along with important client and internal meetings to ensure they had a full understanding of the business. I provided continuous coaching. By the time I departed each role, they were primed and ready to take on my role to ensure the consistency and direction of the strategy we had worked on together. This also meant for a smooth transition for the team.

Needless to say, I am a firm believer in promoting from within when it is possible to do so.

Natalie Brennan and Muffin Break

Muffin Break is a franchised network that opened its first Australian store on the Gold Coast, Australia, in 1989. Today, Muffin Break is a well-known cafe retailer in Australia, New Zealand and the United Kingdom, with over 300 stores internationally and employing over 5000 staff. The business is known for its on-site and homemade quality range of food, and has differentiated itself by ensuring those selected for their individually family-run franchises have value alignment to the brand. Muffin Break has a sister company called Jamaica Blue and both brands are owned by Foodco Group.

Natalie Brennan was the General Manager of Muffin Break for five years – and was with Foodco for an impressive 21 years. Originally training as a teacher (although she never made it to a classroom), Natalie is now a recognised name in franchising after starting in a role at McDonald's. She went on to have a full and remarkable career with many well-known brands, focusing on training and development as well as her passion for sustainability. Like many women, Natalie had challenges along the way with having to overcome industry stereotypes – and has even shared a story from early in her career about how she once lost a job after she was propositioned by a superior. Natalie overcame her challenges by furthering her own education and development, enabling her to position herself in senior roles, determined to pave the way for future women so they were protected from these types of experiences.

Along the way, Natalie has won many accolades and awards:

- Global Top 100 Most Influential Women in Franchising (2020)
- Ranked no.1, Top 30 Franchise Executives (2019)
- Finalist, Premier's Volunteer Recognition Program (2016)
- Franchising Woman of the Year (2015)
- Franchise Woman of the Year, NSW (2015)

Applying the accountability/competency matrix to Muffin Break

While sometimes in leadership it can be tempting to just do a particular task yourself to make sure it's done right, giving staff appropriate levels of accountability and trusting them to do the job goes a long way towards continuing to build their competency – and freeing up your time. However, this trust can only be given when you know as the leader that the existing competency of the employee is at the required level for them to carry out the task successfully.

Muffin Break recognises the importance of building and reinforcing the competencies of their staff members so they can do the roles required of them. Consequently they have a major focus on providing employees the opportunity to undertake nationally accredited training programs. This has the added benefit of ensuring that each store is consistently delivering excellence, which is an important factor in their customer experience differentiation.

In particular, while at Muffin Break, Natalie supported her line managers to ensure they were well equipped with the required resources to train quickly and efficiently. Most importantly, she understood that once her people were sufficiently resourced and therefore competent, she could then trust her people to do their best work – thus she was able to give that accountability when the competency was met.

Top Tips
Leading Your People

Stop and think before you recruit:

- *What's happening:* Often in business, we are juggling a million things and are so understaffed that we don't actually first strategise about the type of person we need to hire. We simply need someone to do a stack of work that is piling up so we hire the first person who looks competent enough to do it, failing to ensure that they are actually a match to us – the employer!

- *How to control it:* Stop, think and plan before you recruit. Now that you are clear on the importance of defining your values (refer to chapter 1), have this top of mind when recruiting. You will get a sense from people when interviewing them if they hold values that align with yours – and if you don't, then you will within the first 90 days of their employ. Use the weighted decision matrix (refer to chapter 5) to apply your thought-out attributes that you need for the role. Be calculated with your decision and guided by your values.

Think of your staff members as Goldilocks:

- *What's happening:* Whether you are interviewing, onboarding or running a typical one-to-one or team meeting, remembering that everything in your team members' environments have to be 'just right' for them to perform at their best. A prospective or new employee will have heightened stress/threat responses coming into a new environment so even more focus must be put on ensuring their environment is one where they can thrive.

- *How to control it:* Plot all staff on a SCARE matrix to understand their domains so you can better understand how to keep their environment in check. If the staff member is new and you aren't sure where they should be plotted, explain SCARE to them and get them to plot themselves. Use your understanding of SCARE to ensure you are keeping all staff, at all times, in the reward state.

Coach to staff members' competencies and natural strengths:

- *What's happening:* Giving staff members more than they can handle to get things off our own to-do list can be tempting. Resist this temptation. Delegating, developing and coaching staff within the limitations of their own competencies is vital for their longevity within your business. Like everything, matching competencies with accountability is a balancing act – staff who are given too little accountability, or are coached on things that aren't their natural interests or strengths, will likely tire and/or bore of you and the role.

- *How to control it:* Use all the models outlined in chapter 6 but be sure to keep the accountability/ competency matrix top of mind. Plot your staff on this matrix monthly, even if just in your head. Think it through and constantly be moving your staff through skill levels to keep their interests and productivity high, within those limitations of their competencies. A steady stream of the right amounts of dopamine, without the fight/flight threat response caused by being in over their head, will help ensure longevity in your business.

>->

>>>

PART III

LEADING YOUR CUSTOMERS

Just like we listen to our staff and develop those relationships to get the best out of our team, we also need to listen to our customers and ensure they feel a connection with us. After all, customers are human too! Women often intuitively know this, and understand that, first and foremost, listening to clients provides the foundation to develop an outstanding customer experience strategy.

The chapters in this part give you the tools to do just that — creating clients who are raving advocates along the way. Two aspects are vital to your success here:

- listening to your customers and developing different touchpoints that enable them to feel connected to your business
- hiring the right staff who understand the importance of the customer experience.

Again, it comes down to having that sense of fun and community and making sure that your customers and clients enjoy themselves, and enjoy speaking and working with your staff — because, ultimately, they are the ones who are developing and nurturing those relationships.

In this part, I outline the Attentive Initiatives that we do in my teams, and just seeing the connections that develop between the staff member and client through this process is, again, another awesome part of my job. Both the staff and client get so much from it — one from giving and one from receiving — and it's just a happy thing to do that people really appreciate.

As part of my MBA, I completed a thesis on differentiation through customer experience that produced a framework to help businesses achieve a sustainable competitive advantage. I now call this my Sustainable Competitive Advantage (SCA) framework, and it acts as the vehicle to engaging and developing a successful customer experience strategy to achieve long-term profitability. I have since put the framework into practice across several of my leadership roles that oversaw the customer experience for the service organisations I worked for.

After completing my thesis, I was fortunate to win the prestige of having my work selected to be presented at the coveted KPMG business breakfast. Only 4 out of 60 graduates achieved this accolade. I've incorporated the research and findings from this thesis into the chapters in this part.

CHAPTER 7

Setting your business apart

These days, many service organisations are finding it increasingly difficult to stand out from their competition, and are becoming largely price-driven in an attempt to do so. This chapter provides an overview of core business strategies relating to differentiation — that is, product, price and customer experience — looking at the advantages and disadvantages of the alternative differentiation strategies. In doing so, I explain why differentiation through customer experience is the most likely to ensure a sustainable competitive advantage by retaining customer loyalty.

In this chapter, I also delve into service design and how identifying your ideal customer is essential when differentiating on customer experience, and help you identify where your key focuses lie from a customer point of view. This is particularly useful if you're operating in a service industry, because you can focus your efforts to ensure greater compatibility when it comes to developing your customer experience processes.

Differentiation strategies

To achieve a competitive advantage, companies differentiate themselves using a variety of strategies—including low cost, product or technology, and customer experience. Differentiation strategies are not a new concept; in fact, these kinds of strategies have been discussed since the 1930s. In this section, I provide an overview of the core differentiation strategies available today, and identify some strengths and weaknesses of each.

Product

In their article 'What is differentiation and how does it work?' marketing experts professors Byron Sharp and John Dawes describe a product differentiation strategy as existing 'when a firm's offering is preferred, on some buying occasions (or by some customers all of the time), over rival firms offerings'. While Sharp and Dawes argue here that differentiation is not a necessary contributor to profitability, they do conclude that differentiation is an almost unavoidable aspect of real competitive markets. However, they also highlight that, while a competitive advantage may come from having a superior product, this advantage is likely to disintegrate over time due to competitors' ability to become more alike — or, basically, copy the product.

More recent research supports the argument that differentiation has now evolved from having a product focus, to having a customer focus.

Examples of a product-led organisation include Apple and Tesla. An Australian example could be Strong Pilates, with their (patent-pending) Rowformer Pilates machine. (See the case study at the end of part IV for more on Strong Pilates.)

Cost

In their best-selling *Exploring Corporate Strategy*, professors Gerry Johnson, Kevan Scholes and Richard Whittington describe low-cost or price strategies (among many others). They outline that, in its simplest form, cost leadership means becoming the lowest cost organisation in a domain of activity. This is the classic 'stack 'em high, sell 'em low' approach, and usually occurs when companies are able to take advantage of economies of scale, (that is, to buy in bulk), which reduces overall costs. However, once what's known as the 'minimum efficient scale' (MES) is reached, very little in the way of further cost reductions is possible, making this strategy risky.

A focus on the lowest price can result in companies entering a price war in a highly competitive market — which is common in the service industry. As a consequence of such a price war, profits can be greatly reduced due to inherent fixed costs on the production side.

Examples of low-cost companies with high product turnover include IKEA and Costco.

Customer experience

In their article 'Total customer engagement: designing and aligning key strategic elements to achieve growth' marketing experts Christopher Roberts and Frank Alpert highlight study findings that 95 per cent of executives believed customer experience was the next competitive battle ground. And this was back in 2010! Up until now, however, in order to compete, many industries have chosen to increase product choice — including increasing features and functions — and this has often resulted in confusion for the average consumer.

To compete successfully in the emerging business environment, current research is suggesting that value to a consumer can be co-created from an experience point of view. This allows customers to actively co-create their own experience through a personalised interaction. When this happens, the co-creation experience is seeded in the experience of the individual, rather than the technology of any given product or service — which, as an example, is something that Netflix does extremely well! Consequently, the individual becomes an active stakeholder in the product experience, increasing customer loyalty. In addition, moving from one-way communication to focused and interactive two-way communication not only builds on customer relationships but also allows companies to gain in-depth knowledge of their customers. This further solidifies the customer relationship and subsequent customer loyalty — and, therefore, profitability.

Examples of customer experience–led organisations are the Ritz Carlton, Netflix and New Zealand's Z Energy. (See the case study at the end of this part for more on Z Energy.)

Pros and cons of each strategy

Table 7.1 summarises the pros and cons of each differentiation strategy focus, and demonstrates that customer experience has the most pros in terms of ensuring sustainable competitive advantage and, therefore, profitability.

Table 7.1 Summary of the pros and cons of differentiation strategies

Strategy focus	Pros	Cons
Product	• Not generally price sensitive	• Most often competitors have the ability to catch up, rendering this strategy unsustainable
		• Increased features and functions subsequently increase confusion for consumers
Price	• Lowest price achieved by high asset turnover and lowest cost	• Fixed costs renders this strategy risky in terms of gross margins eroded by price wars
		• MES affects profitability and long-term sustainability
Customer experience	• Co-creation of value through customer experience creates customer loyalty and profitability	• Time-consuming to implement
	• Interactive communication provides better understanding of customers' behaviour	
	• Uncertainty around capital commitments is reduced	

Differentiation through customer experience

Differentiation through customer experience is derived from a number of key factors that allow sustainable competitive advantage, customer loyalty and, therefore, profitability to be achieved. These key factors are:

- co-creation of value
- encounter experiences
- employee engagement
- customer relationship strategies.

I cover each of these key factors in the following sections, drawing on some recent research.

Co-creation of value

Co-creation of value, also referred to as 'customer journeys', is a vehicle to build customer loyalty through facilitating a collaborative effort between a supplier and customer. With traditional methods in creating customer value now becoming obsolete, as a leader in today's business world, it's now up to you to co-construct value in order to create experiences that are truly unique to your customers. A number of examples are provided throughout this chapter that will make co-construction become clear.

Co-creation of value allows you to design a strong value proposition. This can occur due to the knowledge that is acquired through the development of the supplier–customer relationship. In their 'Total customer engagement' article,

Roberts and Alpert argue that a strong value proposition is critical to ensure a business can create customer engagement and repeat purchases. Importantly, they also suggest that the design of all internal processes should reflect this value proposition — to ensure complete alignment in not just thinking and saying what a firm will do, but also actually demonstrating this through the customer experiences.

Leonieke Zomerdijk and Christopher Voss in 'Service design for experience-centric services' (from 2010) take this on board and go a step further, suggesting that customers can be influenced throughout the 'customer journey' through what they call 'touchpoints' (see the following section).

Encounter experiences

Encounter experiences and interactions with customers — also known as 'touchpoints' — are a series of experiences designed by you as the service provider to influence a customer's impression of your service and overall business. Conceived by co-creation of value, a well-created encounter is one that enables customers to have their desired experiences, which in turn establishes the high level of customer engagement and satisfaction. These satisfying experiences then lead to strong word-of-mouth marketing — which has been shown to be ten times more effective at resonating with a target audience than marketing experiences through print or television media. In turn, this word-of-mouth marketing has a strong correlation to long-term growth and profitability.

An example of this is the touchpoint program we developed in one of my corporate leadership roles, where each touchpoint in the program was developed based on what clients had already told us they wanted more of — thanks to a survey we had run to gather the data. The touchpoint programs were typically quarterly for existing clients, which meant the client would be contacted four times per year. Specifically, clients had told us they wanted more education that would specifically help them grow their business — sometimes this included education on the services we offered, but sometimes not. So, we developed one of the touchpoints in the program around this offering. Once every other quarter, we would research something that was going to specifically help that client grow their business. It could be an article we found online, or it could be a new service offering within our company. The point was we went over and above and looked outside the square of our own service offering to help this client, providing education relevant to them to help them grow their own business.

The perspective of Zomerdijk and Voss (2010) is the most helpful, due to the depth their study goes into regarding the focus of humanistic encounters, or 'clues' as they describe them. They highlight that every interaction or touchpoint a customer experiences with a company provides a clue to the customer on what the business is all about. Customers gather these clues to ultimately determine their overall impression of the business. In their focus on using these clues, touchpoints and encounters to build an emotional connection with the customer, Zomerdijk and Voss argue that a correlation is made with profitability, because of repeat purchases.

In their 1989 article 'The nuts and bolts of formulating differentiation strategy', Gary Getz and Frederick Sturdivant focus most strongly on a business's ability to implement such a strategy. This is equally as important to keep in mind as emotional connection and internal culture, to ensure deliverability as well as profitability.

Employee engagement

Employee interactions are a crucial determinant of customer satisfaction, so effective staff selection for your customer service roles is vital. This is particularly true in service businesses where the touchpoints, or 'moments of truth', are frequent and typically involve more than one transaction. As discussed in the previous section, customers gather clues about a company at every interaction, and use these clues to determine their overall customer experience. Importantly, employees supply many of these clues through their gestures, comments, dress and tone of voice. Consequently, perceived employee effort is often seen as more important in customer satisfaction than the actual abilities of the employee. This suggests that customers are usually satisfied as long as they are communicated with on any service issues to ensure transparency.

Many experts in this area argue that employee engagement is crucial in any customer experience differentiation strategy. Getz and Sturdivant go as far as to say a customer experience strategy will be 'doomed to fail' without it. And Roberts and Alpert (in 'Total customer engagement'), argue that the internal culture is a key enabler in delivering a distinct value proposition. Zomerdijk and Voss (in 'Service design for experience-centric services') also support strong employee engagement, highlighting that employees connecting with customers on a personal and, therefore, emotional level influences the customer's perceived quality of the firm. Consequently, customer satisfaction is increased.

Clearly, to ensure long-term growth, a firm must have not only engaged customers, but also engaged employees.

Customer relationship strategies

Customers come with highly individualised experiences, requirements and expectations, and so it is important to consider the relationship strategies you and your team undertake, and the value of customising each encounter to each customer, to extract maximum value out of the relationship. If you don't ensure relationships are managed in a conscious manner, they can become problematic and unprofitable.

As an example of customising encounters, in our first 18 months of owning my Laser Clinics Australia franchise, we were in the client acquisition phase — that is, growing our client base. One of the things we did to capitalise on each new encounter with each new client was to provide a small gift and a handwritten card welcoming this client into the clinic. This was highly individualised — we personalised the handwritten cards to the client from a specific therapist. When we moved into becoming more of an established clinic, we swapped this strategy to our Attentive Initiatives strategy, which you can find out more about in chapter 8.

The overriding aim of a relationship strategy is to increase relationship value. In *Customer Relationship Management: Creating competitive advantage through win–win relationship strategies*, marketing researchers Kaj Storbacka and Jarmo

Lehtinen outline the Zipper strategy as being a key relationship strategy for managing co-creation of value. The Zipper strategy is a partnership approach where the customer and service provider adapt their processes to each other so that they interlock in the manner of a zipper.

An example of this in action in my current business is when I invited six clients to lunch to work through any blind spots we might have in the clinic. I had 10 questions that I printed out and placed on the table — such as, 'Is there anything you would change if it were your clinic?' and 'As an existing client, what makes you feel valued?' Throughout the lunch, if anyone thought of an answer they would write their response down on a sticky note and hand it to me. This was great because it made the lunch quite informal, while still allowing me to gather valuable data. One of the bits of feedback we received was to include a pager system. This meant that when a client is under an LED light and wants the attention of the therapist, or is ready for their laser hair removal (and, therefore, the therapist may not be in the room with them at that moment), they can simply press a button and it will send an alert to the therapist letting them know the client is ready for or is needing them. So the client is not sitting there waiting for the therapist to come back in or wondering how to get their attention; instead, the client is in control of that moment, which is what they want — especially when sitting there feeling vulnerable half naked waiting for a Brazilian laser treatment!

The aim of this strategy is to achieve a seamless fit and a catalyst for co-creation. This strategy ensures that the encounters and activities occur in the right order so no mismatch in communication occurs.

Bringing the key factors together

Ensuring the development of customer engagement through the co-construction or co-creation of value creates an opportunity for a customer to become naturally entrenched within your business because they are able to engage in personal interaction. Ultimately, this likely increases their loyalty to your business. By identifying desirable customer experiences you and your team can tailor customer encounters or 'touchpoints' as a way to influence your customers' overall impression of the service you provide and your business.

The leading indicators of a customer's impression and, therefore, satisfaction come from the people you employ to carry out customer service roles. So you need employee engagement in any strategy. Further, in order to manage customer loyalty, the strategies you develop and implement need to be adaptable, so they can be made as individual as the customers themselves.

 **PRODUCTIVITY TIP**

An approach that is collaborative and customised for your customers is more likely to ensure that relationship value is extracted from both sides. This situation has shown to solidify and entrench the customer relationship, making it less likely that the customer will want to switch to a different provider or business. And keeping customers is always more productive than finding new ones.

Additional strategies

A winning customer-focused strategy and business plan should cover several other areas. I outline two of the most important in the following sections.

Identifying your ideal client

Identifying your ideal client is really important. Doing so ensures all your marketing and any other relevant strategies are speaking directly to that ideal client, increasing your chance of attraction and conversion. That's not to say you shouldn't also speak to the other identified clients (non-shaded in table 7.2, overleaf), because you can also focus campaigns on attracting these customers too. It just means the majority of your marketing spend is going on the majority of the target market.

In table 7.2, I outline four distinct markets for an aesthetics business. The first column (shaded) represents the 'ideal client'. This client is the main target market for the services provided by the business, and has a higher disposable income so is more likely to select the full-service options. They're also after convenience, so this business being in their local mall increases the chance of not only one visit but repeat business. Therefore, this ideal client should be the main focus for most marketing campaigns and for cross-selling opportunities.

Table 7.2 Identifying your ideal client

	Women aged >35	Women aged <35	Men	Teens
Persona	• Any women over 35 in any industry or profession • Typically 40–60 age category • Concerned with pigmentation, more prominent lines	• Any women under 35 in any industry or profession	• Sportsmen – especially cyclists and triathletes • Men who are self-conscious about body hair	• Teens who are self-conscious about acne • Parents of these teens
Customer objectives	• Quick, affordable and convenient location for all skin, laser and anti-ageing needs • Trusted brand without having to do too much research	• Slow aging process • Affordable and trusted brand	• Permanent solution for hair removal where clinic is accessible and convenient to get to • Affordable	• Teens: eradication of acne to improve self-confidence • Parents: full trust in a known brand
Product offering	• Laser (hair and pigmentation) • Injectables (anti-wrinkle and fillers) • Skin treatments • Coolsculpting	• Laser hair removal • Skin treatments	• Laser hair removal • Injectables (anti-wrinkle and fillers)	• Skin treatments – acne treatments, Kleresca

Voice of Customer research

Voice of Customer (VoC) research is where you gather customer feedback about their experiences with and expectations for your products or services across a variety of mediums. This research allows you to plan how you are going to communicate with and continue to gather information from your customer base — and ties in perfectly with the Zipper Strategy (refer to the 'Customer relationship strategies', earlier in this chapter). A clear and structured VoC program complements the SCA framework (see chapter 8) beautifully, because it links in with phase four — continuous improvement. Combining these approaches helps you ensure your customer experience strategy is sustainable.

In table 7.3, I outline some examples of how you can incorporate VoC research into your overall customer service strategy.

Table 7.3 Voice of Customer research options

Medium	Description	Frequency
Feedback forms	An email sent immediately following a service encounter to a client to ensure we capture any feedback – good or bad. If bad, remedy asap – including a handwritten note from owner. If good, refer a friend initiative introduced and captured.	One email per client per service encounter.
	Direct objective: To quickly remedy issues as they arise to protect against bad reviews.	

(continued)

Table 7.3 (continued)

Medium	Description	Frequency
CHS survey/NPS	Customer Happiness Survey (CHS) and Net Promoter Score (NPS) used to measure the client's customer experience by employee, and provide useful data for continuous improvement. Data to be used as a metric linked to employee performance incentives. *Direct objective:* Internal measurement tool to maintain superior customer service.	Quarterly
Focus groups	A personal invitation sent to five to six clients every six months for a facilitated working lunch where we will seek to uncover any weaknesses, improvements or blind spots of the business. *Direct objective:* To drive focused attention towards areas that matter to our clients, ensuring continuous improvement.	Twice yearly

CHAPTER 8
The Sustainable Competitive Advantage framework

The Sustainable Competitive Advantage (SCA) framework is a combination of all the best bits of the models and theories outlined in chapter 7 and my MBA thesis research. This framework, outlined in table 8.1 (overleaf), provides a clear and concise structure so you can methodically work your way through each phase.

Table 8.1 The Sustainable Competitive Advantage framework

Categories	Subcategories
Phase 1: Service encounters	Event/touchpoint creation from data-driven insights
	Resources/capabilities viability audit
	Economic viability audit
	Functional heads – sign off
Phase 2: Value proposition (VP)	Cross-functional development of VP
	Governance team created if applicable
	Touchpoint program established
	Employee development linked to a tertiary qualification relevant to VP
	Employee performance metric designed to align to VP
Phase 3: Internal culture	Hire happy/positive people and develop them into the role
	Employee engagement of VP
	Touchpoints for all employees in line with VP
	Job description alignment to VP
Phase 4: Measurement	Monthly customer survey – standard set of questions in line with VP
	Continuous improvement in line with VP
Business traits	Recognition and development program developed from key business traits – empirical creativity, fanatical discipline, productive paranoia

SCA framework in theory

In the following sections I run through the theory behind my SCA framework. Later in this chapter, I outline how the framework can be applied in practice.

Phase 1: Service encounters

You and your team using a co-creation of value model to help you design service encounters — that is, co-creating the customer experience with the customer — can help to establish a clear picture of the customer's needs and wants. In other words, it helps take away any guesswork. When you design these service encounters or 'events' with the purpose of maximising the dramatic effect on the customer experience, you create more emotional connection for the customer, which often translates into repeat purchases and positive word-of-mouth publicity by the customer. In turn, this influences increasing profitability. In my current business, 70 per cent of new clients are derived from word-of-mouth marketing. This results in tangible gains on my profit and loss as less revenue is spent on advertising and marketing.

Taking a customer experience–based approach means you can start to build a clear picture of the service encounters your customers want. This can be followed by an assessment of the businesses capabilities and resources, and how these can be strategically directed to ensure the customer's needs are being, and can continue to be, fulfilled.

If you're a leader in a larger business, ensure all functional heads of the business are involved at the earliest opportunity to objectively assess whether the business can implement the activities you've identified as being required to meet the needs of your customers. This can uncover any organisational and cultural roadblocks that could potentially hinder an organisation's path to success. The importance of cross-functional relationships for the implementation of a differentiation strategy is emphasised in Storbacka and Lehtinen's *Customer Relationship Management* (refer to chapter 7). They highlight all functional departments of a business must be aligned to be truly customer centric.

After assessing whether your desired customer service encounters are viable based on the capabilities of the business, the economic viability must also be assessed — that is, you need to determine if the proposed activities make sense financially.

Phase 2: Value proposition

Again, cross-functional participation is critical when developing the value proposition for customers, because it ensures company-wide buy-in and effective communication of the value proposition. In larger businesses, at this stage a governance team is usually created (often including all the functional heads of a business) along with establishing a time line those functional departments will adhere to, to ensure the strategy stays on track. Commonly at this point any performance metrics on the new strategy will be designed by all the functional heads together.

Phase 3: Internal culture

As emphasised in the previous chapter, for your customer experience strategy to be successful, you need employee engagement. Employees are effectively the people delivering the value proposition, so ensuring employees are fully engaged in the process is critical.

One way to engage your employees right from the start is to invite staff to participate in the creation of the customer engagement process. This can prove to be a valuable avenue for a company to explore, because it can equip staff with the flexibility to brainstorm and create innovative customer experiences. You can also implement a process where every employee — no matter their role — engages in a customer touchpoint in some way, rather than this just being confined to frontline staff. An example of this might be a quarterly Voice of Customer (refer to chapter 7) function where non-frontline staff are invited (on rotation) so they also are involved in meaningful customer touchpoints. For this process to be most effective, you would need to ensure job descriptions are aligned with the value proposition concept and include a set of required activities to promote this as such.

Phase 4: Measurement

You need to have measurement tools in place to evaluate the new differentiation strategy. Tools such as surveys and feedback forms can help you evaluate both the customer engagement level and the internal team's engagement. Measurement at the customer level can be further enhanced by including recommendations or testimonials and an assessment of customer loyalty. Whether you've seen an increase in customer revenue can also be assessed here. At the same time, you can measure internal staff behaviour via peer processes and also via customer feedback in order to determine staff alignment with the value proposition.

Creating processes that encourage staff to develop initiatives against the planned customer experience are also beneficial. This allows for continuous improvement based on customer feedback and gives staff an avenue to easily implement improvements as required.

Incorporating three key business traits

Successfully undertaking the preceding process is only part of the journey for an effective customer differentiation strategy. To ensure your strategy continues on its road to success after implementation, you must incorporate the three key business traits emphasised in the classic business book *Great by Choice* by Jim Collins and Morten Hansen. The three clear business traits are empirical creativity, fanatic discipline and productive paranoia.

Collins and Hansen describe empirical creativity as not necessarily being the most creative company, but being creative enough to succeed and make bold moves while limiting risks. Fanatical discipline is your business demonstrating mental independence, in that it remains consistent in the face of social pressures and resists the instinct to 'follow the herd'. Productive paranoia is where, as a business, you prepare for the worst-case scenario, which effectively puts you in a protected position in the event of a disruptive situation, minimising the effect on the business.

SCA framework in practice

In my senior leadership career, I worked for a large corporate in Australia, and my department looked after retaining the small-to-medium enterprise (SME) customers for Australia and New Zealand. I used my SCA framework as the basis of our strategy and it provided a clear customer-led strategy for us to prosper from.

I split the framework into three key sections delivered over three horizons of time, as shown in figure 8.1.

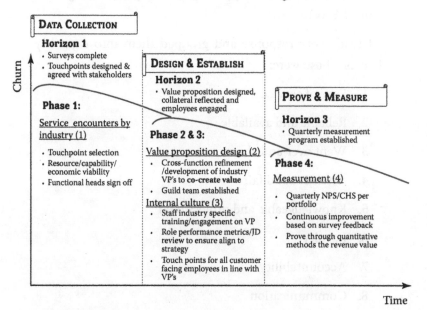

Figure 8.1 The SCA framework in practice

Data collection

In this phase, all we wanted to do was gather data from clients and really listen to what they had to say. To gather sufficient data to really give us a clear picture, I had a question inserted in the annual NPS survey that went out to all the SME clients. We simply asked, 'Tell us about the best client experience you have ever had — what made it so great?' From the responses, we were able to create a shortlist of meaningful customer touchpoint ideas.

We received 1746 written responses from people wanting to tell their story. The marketing manager at the time was shocked we got so many — he had expected people to just ignore the question altogether due to them having to write an actual response, as opposed to simply answering on a scale of 1 to 10.

I read every response and grouped them into eight key themes. These were:

1. Ease of service

2. Reliable and available

3. Went over and above

4. Attentive and fair

5. Knowledgeable and professional

6. Loyalty

7. Accountability

8. Communication

From this information we were able to create a thorough value proposition that centred on what they told us they needed: to proactively support our customers through meaningful communication. This value proposition included three touchpoint programs that each included key 'tiny memorable moments'. These moments were effectively co-created with our clients, from them having told us what was important to them in the survey. This, in turn, significantly increased the chances of our clients becoming raving advocates. We called these tiny memorable moments our Attentive Initiatives. (More on what these three touchpoints were, and some examples of our Attentive Initiatives, in the following section.)

Interestingly, Natalie Brennan, former General Manager of Muffin Break, spearheaded customer experience strategies that were led by this very idea: data collection from clients. This led to their gluten-free range.

The birth of our Attentive Initiatives came about through one of the responses that has always stuck with me. A survey respondent described an experience they'd had when they had been test-driving a car. The car salesperson and the buyer were chatting about music and what they liked after a particular song had come on the radio. The person ending up buying the car and, when the new car was delivered to the buyer, a CD (yes it was CDs back then) of the band the buyer had said he liked was in the CD player in the car. The car salesperson had gone out and especially purchased the CD for the client and had it in the car ready for him.

PRODUCTIVITY TIP

When you or a staff member goes over and above what a client is expecting, it causes a highly impactful positive emotional response, and this causes a long-term memory to be formed. This emotional memory is implanted deep into the brain (in the hippocampus), as opposed to the fleeting thoughts in the prefrontal cortex. It is this emotional bank that solidifies the opportunity and fluency of positive word-of-mouth discussions – and makes your and your team's jobs easier.

Design and establish

The three touchpoint programs that made up our value proposition for this strategy were as follows:

1. An onboarding touchpoint program to ensure new clients fully understood all the opportunities that were available to them with their subscription.

2. A quarterly touchpoint program that covered existing customers to ensure they were kept abreast of any new technologies being introduced that could help their respective businesses.

3. A VIP touchpoint program that focused in on the higher spending clients to ensure support was provided at a more intensified and appropriate level.

These touchpoint programs covered all clients, and were supported with a comprehensive digital plan, to ensure each group was looked after in a methodical and tenacious approach. Most importantly, these touchpoints helped ensure the customers felt supported in a meaningful way and, thus, we lived up to our value proposition.

One example of an Attentive Initiative we used in this team was when my staff member and their client connected over both being from New Zealand. My staff member followed up by sending the client a NZ coffee mug full of NZ lollies. This was a relatively inexpensive gesture, especially in terms of the dramatic effect it had on the client. The emotional connection formed by this customer that linked to the service we provided was significant, and further secured and grew our business with that particular customer.

To ensure the internal culture reflected the value proposition design — that is, we had employee engagement as well — new commission plans were designed and established, customer portfolios were re-classified, portfolios were re-allocated to appropriate staff, new job descriptions were designed, and training calendars were established and rolled out.

In addition, a cross-functional group (governance team) was created to ensure appropriate levels of buy-in across the business were adhered to, to ensure the best chance of success for the new value proposition.

Prove and measure

To prove and measure the value proposition on an ongoing basis, we established a quarterly continuous improvement plan based on the ongoing quarterly survey feedback we received.

We worked off the same metrics each quarter for continuity, and these were NPS, Client Happiness Score (CHS) and churn (where customers stop using your company's product or service). We also created specific reports to allow us to stay ahead of the curve. A 'Warning signs of churn' report, for example, allowed us to pre-empt churn and be proactive.

Keep in mind that you can also use your customer feedback to gain online public reviews. As an example from my current Laser Clinics Australia franchise, we try to take advantage of our NPS results. Each of our clients receives a NPS customer feedback email following a visit to the clinic. If they send in feedback, it comes just to me as the owner privately. If the feedback is positive (and, of course, it always is!), I then reply to them asking if they would mind making their feedback public with a Google review. They are usually only too happy to do so, and I make it easy for them by providing a link straight to the appropriate page for them to write their review. This small step in my daily process has meant, at the time of writing, my clinic has 500 per cent more five-star Google reviews than any other clinic of the same age.

Z Energy

I absolutely adore, Z Energy – an organisation in New Zealand that succeeded in rising above their competition in a severely price-driven market to become the most preferred brand for petrol in New Zealand in under three years following their rebranding exercise (when Shell sold off their NZ operations in 2011). As a petrol provider, Z Energy operates in a highly competitive market where differentiation is extremely challenging to achieve and sustain.

Z Energy now has over 2500 employees and over 200 petrol stations across New Zealand. When taking over the petrol operations from Shell and rebranding, Z Energy surveyed 17 000 New Zealanders to help develop their strategy and ensure the value proposition that was delivered was on point.

Applying the SCA framework to Z Energy

The customer touchpoints Z Energy has implemented make them stand out from their competition, and also provide us with some insights into how profitability may have been achieved from this. Z Energy also implemented key activities with employees to ensure a company-wide buy-in of the strategy and successful execution.

Service encounters

Service encounters allow a company to reveal what is most important to customers to build a value proposition around these needs and wants. Z Energy CEO Mike Bennetts summarised this when he stated, 'We listened carefully to customers and we have developed a brand and an offer which is all about our customers'. This is proven in touchpoint experiences such as the friendly staff, forecourt concierge, speed of service and better coffee and food.

All these examples connect with customers on a personal and emotional level – whether it be a customer appreciating the speed of service, appreciating the coffee (which is not usually something coupled with a petrol station and saves that customer from having to make two stops) or, simply, a friendly and helpful staff member engaging in conversation. This is meaningful because these touchpoints stimulate the emotional connections that research suggests are the drivers for repeat business and, therefore, a sustainable competitive advantage.

Value proposition

The value proposition when aligned to service encounters allows a company to emanate exactly what a customer wants, increasing chances of repeat purchase and positive word of mouth. Z Energy employee skills are continually developed in providing an outstanding retail customer experience, linking this with a customer experience value proposition. This development could occur through a tertiary qualification, for example.

Z Energy has created its value proposition from listening to customers. The company constantly improves their offering by having active ongoing forums via platforms such as Facebook and Twitter for their customers to provide feedback. This helps ensure the offering is always relevant to their audience. Z Energy even goes as far as not just taking the feedback but also responding to each person who provides it with a personal thank you message, further engaging with their audience on a personal and emotional level. Back in 2013, their 'What do you reckon?' promotion – where they gave people the opportunity to add their ideas on what Z Energy could do next on a dedicated Facebook page and website – was another example of how Z Energy is on the forefront of learning all they can about their customers' needs, wants and ideas.

Internal culture

Having the right internal culture ensures the employees themselves are engaged and, within their own capacity, are responsible for delivering the value proposition offering. Z Energy has a training facility in place when bringing on new employees, and this does more than just train them on the role they're being brought in to do. It also empowers them to the point they feel proud when they put on their Z Energy uniform. One staff member even went as far as saying she felt like her 'Z vest' was her superman cape due to what the Z Energy brand represents and what she was trained to do. This shows Z Energy actively engages employees and has touchpoints for all employees in the execution of their value proposition.

In terms of job description alignment to the value proposition, Z Energy has very clear expectations of their staff that certainly align with their value proposition and is very simply kept in line with their key values. These expectations are as follows:

- *Stand out:* Build a better business and better world.
- *Speak up:* Extraordinary outcomes are fuelled by active participation and dialogue.
- *Side by Side:* Learning and growing together delivers unlimited potential.

The one clear observation of Z Energy with hiring their people – and arguably the reason they are as successful as they are in customer service – is they hire 'happy and positive people' above all else. This ties in well to the part of their strategy on 'linking employee development to tertiary qualifications'. People can be developed; however, attitudes and personalities are much harder to change.

Measurement

Measurement is critical to ensure a value proposition is just as relevant now as it was when it was created. Monitoring that the value proposition is being properly executed is also vital. Z Energy has a rigorous process in place to ensure their value proposition is monitored, which includes surveying 400 random people each month asking the same standard set of questions (which align to their value proposition). Z Energy also obtains customer feedback and carries out continuous improvement of their value proposition on a daily (if not hourly basis) through their Facebook and Twitter offerings.

Business traits

The three business traits of empirical creativity, fanatic discipline and productive paranoia are certainly validated by Z Energy. Empirical creativity is evident in their approach to customer experience and how vigilant they have been in listening to their customers through platforms such as Facebook and Twitter and aiming to fulfil customer needs to the best of their ability. What is even better is that they act quickly on this customer feedback, and this creates the emotional connections with customers that build long-term loyalty. Fanatical discipline and production paranoia is evident in the rigorous measurement of performance through extensive customer surveys completed monthly. This ensures Z Energy is always at the forefront of what the customers are actually experiencing day-to-day and acts accordingly as needed.

Top Tips
Leading Your Customers

Identify your core strategy for your business:

- *What's happening:* Without clearly defining your core business strategy, you can be left vulnerable to drifting in your market and changing directions like the wind. When this happens, it is challenging to gain the traction and grit required to become a successful and high-performing business. We are all in business to make money; however, the avenue you take to do this is dependent on your businesses core strategy. Are you wanting to develop the very best-in-market product like Apple and Tesla? Do you pride yourself on having the lowest cost furniture in town, like Ikea? Or do you want to be known for your exemplary customer experience that has your clients raving about you long after they've walked out of the shop or business?

- *How to control it:* Assuming it is the customer experience route you would like to take (and you've got to the end of this part), you are ready to implement your own version of the SCA framework, starting with truly listening to your customers. Once you have clarity and determination to provide the best customer experience that will differentiate you from your competitors, the experiences your clients get will radiate out of your business through your hand-picked and perfectly aligned team, and the watertight processes you have put in place to ensure your success in creating raving advocate clients.

Identify what your clients care most about in terms of service and build your value proposition around that:

- *What's happening:* In your day-to-day operations of your business, you may think you know what your clients want – but have you ever actually asked them? It may not be what you think. You may think they want you to simply provide the service your business does – such as laser hair removal or skin treatments, for example – but any old beauty salon or laser clinic can do this too, so what makes you stand out? Remember Z Energy is just a petrol station, but it's what they do in those service encounters that make them stand out.

- *How to control it:* Following the SCA framework's phases 1 and 2 will enable you to become very clear on what is most important to your clients, and develop your value proposition, processes and team around these new enlightenments.

Identify your ideal client and establish clear communication channels with them:

- *What's happening:* Many businesses simply sell to whomever will buy from them, and that's not wrong – a sales a sale – but what if you could increase your total number of customers by speaking directly to your ideal client market through targeted and carefully crafted marketing messaging? When you are clear on who your ideal client is, your ability to bring in more like-for-like clientele increases due to your thorough understanding of their profile.

- *How to control it:* Working through the Additional strategies in chapter 7 will provide you a template to follow for your own business. It is important to note that sharing with your ideal client what it is you do is not actually the goal here i.e. laser treatments, skin treatments etc. However, matching what you do in language that aligns with their customer objective is where the magic is. In this example, 35+ year old mums are busy, they are usually working to a budget, and if they can get their laser (or skin or injectable treatment) done while out doing their other errands, it's a win. So this needs to be kept in mind when communicating with this market – focusing on the way the offering is quick, affordable and in a convenient location. This increases the chances of higher sales with like-for-like customers because you are speaking their language in terms of what's important to them.

PART IV

>>>

LEADING YOUR BUSINESS

While I personally love strategy, reports and tracking my numbers, I know many people don't. If you're one of them, don't skip this part! Yes, this part is the sensible and somewhat dry part of the book. In parts I, II and III, I focused on emotional connections and relationships and what women tend to be naturally good at. The focus in this part is on the more analytical aspects of your leadership; however, the information here can help set you up for success through protection, so you're not wasting your time and energy — and your or your business's money — on investing in dud industries or markets.

The models and ratios in this part can help you ensure that your investment is protected, and your business is protected going forward by measuring against industry benchmarks. You can set yourself up to regularly check that everything is as it should be and, if it's not, you're informed and can do something about it. The financials may be your least favourite part of the job, but think of it like business hygiene — it's just a necessity.

If I had bought my clinic in the geographical area I first was looking at, I may have been bankrupt by now — especially with COVID wreaking havoc on everyone's lives. But because I ran through Porter's Five Forces (one of the models you will learn about in chapter 9) prior to investing, I was alerted to the full competitor activity and saturation in the area. Although the industry was still a safe and great one to invest in, learning about this when I did, protected me from investing in the wrong geographical spot.

I discuss the importance of knowing your own personal values right at the beginning of part I. When your values align with the values of your business, you are much more likely to find yourself in the sweet spot of productivity. Doors open and you are what I often refer to as 'in the current'. Swimming in (or with) the current rather than against makes all aspects of your life easier — work is easier, relationships are easier, and you are ultimately more successful in all your endeavours. Conversely, you certainly know when you are swimming against the current, too; life is just harder, more convoluted and unenjoyable, and you seem to be coming up against hurdle after hurdle. I bet just reading this you have examples that are popping into your head of when you were swimming against the current.

If considering a business investment opportunity — perhaps buying a franchise business — ask yourself, does this company or business appreciate the same things I do? Along with overarching values, consider other aspects too — whether that be innovative technology, marketing slickness, operational excellence or world-class customer experience. You want to admire what it is they do and how they do things. You want to make sure there is value alignment. Be selective of who you tie your name to — again, knowing your own values up front takes away a lot of pain later.

I have had many alignments in my career, and many misalignments. One of my most exceptional alignments, and the best thing I ever did, was buy into the Laser Clinics

Australia franchise due to the company sharing the same values I did. I have done nothing but flourish — even in the face of bush fires, a global pandemic, border closures and floods. My business has had all but the kitchen sink thrown at it, and we have not just survived but come through it happy, more resilient and prospering. The support the franchisor provided throughout was second to none, proving them to be an excellent partner, which is an important factor to look for when selecting who you will work for or with — whether that's an employer, a business partner or a franchisor.

CHAPTER 9

Strategic models for business and finance

When I bought into my franchise, I did not come from the industry the franchise operated in so I needed to learn a lot before I could ascertain if this was a good business opportunity. Value alignment was vital, but I also needed to know my money was not going to go down the drain due to macro- and micro-economic factors.

Any time in my career that I have needed to, I have utilised three business models to guide my strategic business level decisions. These are PESTEL, SWOT and the Porter's Five Forces. I outline these models in this chapter, and also run through some quick financial ratios.

Business models

No doubt you've used or learnt about SWOT analysis at some point in your career, but perhaps you're less sure what PESTEL is and how it ties into SWOT. A SWOT analysis developed off the back of a PESTEL analysis is more thorough and detailed. Applying a Porter's Five Forces analysis then allows you to look at the even bigger picture.

When you are making large business-level decisions where a lot of money is at stake, you certainly want the thorough and holistic view that PESTEL, SWOT and Porter's Five Forces provides.

In the following sections, I outline how I used these models in the context of deciding whether I would buy a business in the aesthetics industry and, if so, where. If you're a leader or owner within an existing business, you can also use a similar approach when considering whether to enter new markets or take on competitors with a new product.

PESTEL

PESTEL was developed over 50 years ago by Francis Aguilar and stands for Political, Economic, Sociological, Technical, Environmental and Legal. So this analysis looks for macro factors that could pose opportunities or threats to your local business. Again, applying PESTEL first makes for a more informed SWOT analysis.

When deep diving into each of the PESTEL domains, you can uncover macro-economic issues that could positively or negatively affect your industry. These are things outside of your control so are definitely things you want eyes on.

Table 9.1 provides an example of the PESTEL I did when entering the aesthetic industry in 2019. I found the information included in this analysis via my online research into two vital reports: *Cosmetic Lasers Market—Global Industry Analysis, Size, Share, Growth, Trends, and Forecast 2018–2026* (www.researchandmarkets.com) and *Aesthetic Lasers Market—Global Forecast 2028* (www.reportsanddata.com).

Table 9.1 PESTEL analysis of the aesthetic industry

Political	Economic
• Strict regulations are projected to ensure increased device efficiency without adverse effect	• Lower interest rates are resulting in higher disposable income
• WA law changes have seen a surge of laser clinics opening there	• Forecasted growth of $798M in 2018 to $1.93B in 2026 worldwide; compound annual growth 11.3%
	• Asia–Pacific is the fastest growing region for aesthetics industry
	• Rising population of baby boomers have high levels of disposable incomes as reaching retirement

(continued)

Table 9.1 (continued)

Sociological	Technological
• Increasing geriatric/baby boomer population	• New technologies in cosmetic medicine = new products
• Rising medial tourism industry	
• Young people are opting for cosmetic procedures earlier to slow the process of ageing	• Growth in medical sciences
• 43% increase in male participation over 5 years to 2018	• Needle-free procedure technological advances have boosted rate of treatment adoption
• Growing awareness and changing concepts of beauty are main drivers of growth	• Do-it-yourself at home devices also becoming available, posing some threat
• Conventional hair removal treatments are time-consuming and in fast-moving lifestyle they are no longer feasible for many	
• Permanent solution in hair removal is increasing the popularity, especially considering savings over a 20-year period of $7968	
• Misconceptions associated still with cosmetic surgeries can reduce demand, hampering/slowing market growth	

Environmental	Legal
• Increased global warming is resulting in increased skin damage, in turn increasing demand for aesthetics industry	• QLD requires a laser tech certification; NSW not required
	• NSW facing harsher regulations due to a legal case
	• Medical negligence cases are a threat

SWOT

As I'm sure you're aware, a SWOT analysis looks at Strengths, Weaknesses, Opportunities and Threats. The SWOT I was able to produce off the back of the PESTEL analysis (refer to table 9.1) was far richer than if I had simply looked at micro-economic or localised factors concerning the business. A SWOT on its own can leave you vulnerable to macro-economic factors that you hadn't considered.

Table 9.2 provides the SWOT analysis I completed once I started to look at specific franchise business options in the aesthetics industry.

Table 9.2 SWOT analysis of specific franchise business in the aesthetic industry

Strengths	Weaknesses
• Forecasted growth of 'booming' aesthetics industry looks to be sustainable due to law changes (e.g. WA) making treatments previously held for higher income families now affordable for average person	• Misconceptions associated with cosmetic surgeries can reduce demand for market, hampering/slowing growth
• Conventional hair removal treatments no longer feasible or desired versus permanent solutions such as laser	• Some brand perception of rushing clients in and out of their treatments
• Needle-free procedures and technological advances have boosted rate of treatment adoption	• Second to market as competitor is already in local mall
• Franchisor has strong brand presence to leverage against	• No personal industry experience
• Franchisor uses only the industry best products	• Not personally living in the area means I am not living in their community (e.g. schools, clubs) so I don't have the relationships built
• Strong customer experience and sales management background	
• Strong leadership skills to foster a high-performing team culture	

(continued)

Table 9.2 (continued)

Opportunities	Threats
• Higher disposable income for consumers due to lower interest rates and baby boomers	• Political changes impacting further regulation could affect profits
• Increasing baby boomer population	
• Young people opting for cosmetic non-surgical procedures to slow the ageing process; also 43% growth in male participation over 5 years – this means the market is getting wider and wider, and no longer traditionally >35-year-old women	• Do-it-yourself at home devices pose threat for some segments in the market
	• Medical negligence is a constant threat given the injectable treatments on offer
• Aesthetics market growth also driven by increased global warming causing some skin damage, resulting in a high population of baby boomers who potentially have skin damage, and who have disposable income to get this fixed	• Second to market as competitor is already in mall
• A methodical customer-centric approach to running the clinic can be applied	• I don't live in the area so accessibility if I need to get to the clinic in a hurry could pose a threat

Porter's Five Forces

Developed in 1979 by Michael Porter, a Porter's Five Forces analysis is a framework that helps you take a wider look than simply your direct competitors. The five forces that make up Porter's model are suppliers, buyers, substitutes, new entrants and competitors. The power and threat of these forces within an industry combine to influence a company's potential profitability.

Originally intended to be used to look at competitor landscape by industry, I used this analysis to look at both the aesthetics industry and how this specifically related to the individual franchise I was considering purchasing.

By investigating buyers, substitutes, new entrants and suppliers, I was able to form a holistic view of microeconomic factors that could affect my business. Table 9.3 shows my Porter's Five Forces analysis.

Table 9.3 Porter's Five Forces analysis of a specific franchise business in the aesthetic industry

Suppliers – moderate risk	Substitutes – moderate risk
• Cost of goods could rise with regulatory changes; however, generally suppliers remain a low risk. • Reliance on key suppliers for certain products could present a risk.	• Several substitutes are available, ranging from cancer clinics to medispas to medical centres to acupuncture clinics in the local area. All pose a substitute risk, although due to the higher price points this is a moderate risk.

Buyers – high risk	New entrants – high risk
• Due to the increased competitor activity in this space, and as popularity and normality continues to grow in cosmetic treatments, buyer power is also increasing, with consumers switching between whichever company has the best offer. To mitigate, delivering outstanding customer experience and building high trust, as well as coupling with a leading franchise, will insulate the business as best we can against this force. • A high volume and highly transactional client base does leave this business exposed to churn more easily. Again, excelling in customer experience will mitigate.	• High trust in existing award-winning brands makes it difficult for new entrants to get established; however, barriers to entry are relatively low making new entrants a higher risk. • High economies of scale ensure prices by big players remain competitive against independents or smaller franchises. However, this does mean a drop in profitability for bigger players by having to compete on price. To mitigate, focus will be on building a sustainable competitive advantage through customer experience to ensure loyalty and growth through word-of-mouth.

(continued)

Table 9.3 (continued)

Competitors – high risk

- Six direct competitors operate in the area with an assumed total of 30 rooms and 30 full-time equivalent (FTE) staff. All clinics being fully booked equates to **1680** people having treatments per week based on one appointment time within each hour per room, and clinics being open for 8 hours per day on average, 7 days per week.

- The total population for target area is 96108 of which 48.3% are men and 51.7% women. If the assumption is made that 65% of the women and 20% of the men in the age brackets of 12–65 are our addressable market, this equates to **34594** people.

- Assuming that clients have treatments at six weekly intervals, the target area has a rate of **73% saturation** prior to opening.

- If we use the same method as above and remove the addressable market restriction to make both the female and male market 100%, saturation **drops to just 32%**.

Understanding the saturation in your market is a critical step. As mentioned, I was looking at another potential geographical area closer to where I lived in my city when I brought my franchise. Obviously, the PESTEL and SWOT showed similar results; however, once I got to this local level of competitor analysis, it quickly became apparent that the area in question was oversaturated and so, back to the drawing board I went until the opportunity came up in the area that was the best fit.

Analysing direct competitors

Once you have the micro- and macro-economic vantage points from the three analysis models, and are closer to settling on a specific location, you can complete a deeper analysis of direct competitors in the area. Table 9.4 shows my analysis of six direct competitors in the area I was looking to invest in.

Table 9.4 Direct competitor analysis

Competitor	Competitor information	Competitive advantage
Competitor #1	• Skin and laser treatments, no injectables	• More products/ services
	• Just two reviews online but both positive and 5/5 stars	• Better consumer confidence
Competitor #2	• Limited opening hours – closed on Sundays, no late nights	• Longer opening hours
	• 3 of the 23 reviews were very concerning about the injecting doctor (i.e. no numbing cream, confusing clients, not discussing price first, over-injecting, bad attitude)	• Better consumer confidence
Competitor #3	• Open only four days per week (closed Mondays, Fridays and Sundays)	• Longer opening hours when open
	• No online reviews for clinic	• Better consumer confidence
Competitor #4	• Closed Sundays and no late nights	• Longer opening hours
	• Limited reviews online (17 Facebook reviews and 2 Google), but reviews are positive	• Better consumer confidence
Competitor #5	• Limited online reviews – 3 Google	• More products/ services
	• Closed Sundays, close at 5 pm each day – no late nights	• Better consumer confidence
	• Do surgical + beauty treatments also	
	• High end of pricing	

(continued)

Table 9.4 (continued)

Competitor	Competitor information	Competitive advantage
Competitor #6	• Weak on communications with their clients • Errors in booking times led to bad review • Higher price point	• Specific acne treatment

Once you have completed all of these analysis models, you can start to prepare a focused and targeted strategy, or business plan.

Using the analysis models from the preceding sections, I created a strategic business plan for my purchase of a Laser Clinics Australia franchise business. I also included aspects of the SCARE model (refer to chapter 4) and my SCA framework (chapter 8). When I met with the franchisor, they told me this business plan was among the best they had seen. It was thorough, and on point. Ultimately, it (and my team) assisted greatly in becoming Franchisee of the Year just two years later.

Financial ratios

As a leader or business owner, you can use many financial ratios to help ensure you are in control of your business. However, to provide some guidance and simplify this minefield, table 9.5 outlines a few of the key ratios I use regularly in the aesthetics industry. Please note that the average percentages included in the table may differ industry to industry, so you should research further to understand the best benchmark for your own business.

Table 9.5 Key financial ratios and how to apply them

Financial ratio	Application
Cost of Goods Sold (COGS) as a Percentage of Revenue Calculation: COGS ÷ revenue × 100	The Cost of Goods Sold (COGS) is the direct cost attributed to the products sold by your business. COGS as a percentage of revenue generally sits at 31% across most industries; however, for my current industry, I work off this being just 18%.
Wage to Sales ratio Calculation: Wages ÷ revenue × 100	Your Wage to Sales ratio can be anything between 10% and 40%, depending on the industry. I work off my wages being no more than 30% of total sales revenue.
COGS and wages combined as a percentage of revenue should equal no more than 50%. Otherwise, these costs are digging too much into your profits.	
Net Profit Margin Calculation: Net Profit ÷ Revenue × 100	While your revenue is the total income your business generated, your net profit is the value that remains after all expenses are subtracted from this revenue. For established small businesses, your Net Profit Margin should sit somewhere between 7 and 10% – which would be considered 'average' in its performance. When you start pushing towards 20%, this would be considered 'good' in terms of performance.
Gross Profit Margin Calculation: (Revenue − COGS) ÷ Revenue × 100	Your Gross Profit Margin is similar to the COGS %, but back to front. A healthy Gross Profit Margin for most businesses would range from 50 to 70%.

Strong Pilates

While reasonably new to the fitness market in Australia (having launched pre-COVID in 2019), Strong Pilates have gained significant momentum, and continue to go from strength to strength (no pun intended)!

Strong Pilates is a franchise business originating in Melbourne, Australia, and founded by Michael Ramsey and Mark Armstrong. Michael and Mark sold six of their successful F45 franchises to fund the venture. At the time of writing, the business has 31 studios across Australia and New Zealand; however, what makes this brand truly exciting is the demand and growth that is in store for them. So far, almost 130 franchise territories have been locked in across Australia and New Zealand already, and they have plans to expand the brand into the United Kingdom, Singapore and Canada.

A key point of difference for the business is their 'Rowformer' machine (patent pending). This machine differs from the more commonly used 'reformer' Pilates machine. What makes the Rowformer different is the rower attached to the Pilates reformer bed, meaning in the various 45-minute workouts purposefully designed by Strong Pilates, you are getting a low-impact (important for many of us as we move into our forties), high-intensity workout that is full of strength, cardio, stability and movement training – suitable for any fitness level. Seizing the opportunity and moving to lock in the US-developed Rowformer patent was an incredibly smart move by the owners of Strong Pilates.

Combining their Rowformer machine with slick technology and marketing, and impeccably consistent customer experiences, Strong Pilates' competitive advantage is likely to be secure for years to come.

Applying Porter's Five Forces to Strong Pilates

As mentioned in chapter 9, the Porter's Five Forces model forces you to look beyond a typical like-for-like competitor – such as the competing gym down the road – and enables you to make informed decisions off the back of your analysis. Applying this model to Strong Pilates uncovers how such a fitness brand could seemingly just pop up out of nowhere and thrive in what appeared to be an already saturated market.

Suppliers

Strong Pilates appears to have just the one supplier in regard to the actual Rowformer machines, which due to the patent application, would make this contract watertight. Therefore, this supplier would be considered a very low risk.

In regard to other suppliers, these are likely to be locally sourced so should also be low risk.

Buyers

Strong Pilates clients, or 'buyers' as the Porter's model categorises them, are typically people who are already paying for both a gym membership for cardio and a Pilates class for stability and strength at a different location. In other words, these potential clients are currently doubling the time commitment and cost to achieve their fitness goals. In a largely time-poor world (especially for working mothers), Strong Pilates succeeds in squeezing both workouts into 45 minutes at a fraction of the time and cost. Most importantly, Strong Pilates is able to maintain the maximum impact the buyer desires. Michael adds to this point well by highlighting, 'Traditionally, Pilates has been an 'upfront' casual or pack model where consumers find themselves paying $25 to $45 per class. Strong Pilates is a membership-based model where our regular clients can pay as little as $8 per class'.

Due to the groundswell Strong Pilates is creating, resulting in a solid membership base, along with the competitive advantage with the Rowformer and the excellent customer experience, loyalty remains high. This means the likelihood of buyers switching, and therefore causing risk to the individual franchises, is low.

New entrants

Due to the patent pending on the Rowformer, Strong Pilates has effectively insulated themselves against any new entrants that could pose a competitive threat into their market. Not many businesses can say this.

Competitors

Following on from the new entrants force, Strong Pilates are reasonably protected in this direct competitor space, again due to the patent pending on the Rowformer. Michael, who won the Fitness category at the 2022 Australian Young Entrepreneur Awards, stated in an interview with Business News Australia, 'I think we fit in a genre where we really have no competition yet we're competition to everyone'.

Substitutes

Strong Pilates has a few substitutes, including more traditional Pilates studios, yoga studios, circuit training studios, CrossFit, F45, and typical gyms – are all active substitutes and each has their place in the market and appeals to different consumers.

For a typical gym owner, Strong Pilates may not have even been in their peripheral vision as a competitive threat. However, when you apply the Porter's Five Forces model, you would need to include them in the Substitutes force. They may not be a direct competitor, but are definitely still worth keeping an eye on. This becomes even more important if you were looking at opening a gym. If, after doing the Porter's model analysis, you uncovered a Strong Pilates business was operating down the road, you may think twice about opening your gym – or you might go and open a Strong Pilates franchise somewhere else instead. These models are there to guide you, so you make informed decisions.

Top Tips
Leading Your Business

Protect your investment:

- *What's happening:* I've seen many people follow passions and jump headfirst into businesses without fully understanding micro- or macro-factors for the industry. This oversight ultimately made success challenging and, consequently, further cash injections were needed to keep the business afloat. Protecting your investment or your business's – whether that be protecting actual dollars invested or protecting the time you and your team have invested – is vital.

- *How to control it:* Utilising the clean sweep of all three models covered in chapter 9 – PESTEL, SWOT and Porter's Five Forces – puts you in the best position to have eyes on everything and everyone who could negatively affect your business and, thus, protect your investment.

Know your competitor landscape but don't obsess over it:

- *What's happening:* No doubt you can name one or two of your fiercest competitors. You know what they do and what they charge, largely because their business model is almost identical to your own. It is important to know who and where your competitors are, but once you know, put that knowledge up on the shelf unless something develops that makes it absolutely necessary to take down again. What is more important to focus on is your competitor landscape in terms of your runway – that is, how big is your market and how much is already saturated.

- *How to control it:* Working through Porter's Five Forces in much the same way I did in chapter 9 will provide clarity on your competitor landscape, and gauge your market saturation. If doing this exercise uncovers a significant runway in a particular service for a particular ideal client, sing that from the rooftop to attract those clients to you through your marketing messaging. Don't worry about what your competitors are doing – you are smarter, you are focusing on controlling your controllables. Stay in your bubble and keep going with small, consistent and daily tasks until you and your team hit your goals.

Measure your business monthly with industry benchmarked financial ratios:

- *What's happening:* You can get so busy working 'in' your business that you might forget to take stock to ascertain if you are running it right from a financial point of view. Knowing your numbers – whether you own your business or are a leader in a larger business – is extremely vital! Even when you get to the stage of working 'on' your business rather than in it, you may think you are working on it because you finally have time to work more closely on that marketing or people project that you've been meaning to get to. However, this is still in effect working in the business. Working on the business needs to take you higher than anything functional to give you a birds-eye view of where strings need to be pulled for better overall financial performance. One of the ways to do this is through industry appropriate benchmarks, such as financial ratios.

- *How to control it:* Find financial ratios that are relevant to your business and become familiar with any industry benchmarks. Measure these ratios monthly. If, for example, your Wage to Sales ratio is trending too high, you know that you need to look closer at your underperforming staff and pull the appropriate levers of either additional training or exiting them from the business. If your COGS % is trending too high, you know you need to keep a closer watch on costs and rein in any over-the-top spending. Financial ratios don't lie, so you keeping track of them allows you to always know exactly where you stand.

CONCLUSION

>>>>>>>>>>>>>>>>>>>>>>>>>>>>>>>>>>>

We've covered a lot of practical content in this book. We worked through the importance of knowing your values, and aligning these to help guide your business decisions, your team, your culture and yourself. We explored not just how to control your environment, but also why this is so important for our future selves. And hopefully you've gained some insight into imposter syndrome and how this can be managed.

I introduced you to the leadership styles included in VACAS and outlined why each are vital under different circumstances. And we looked at the SCARE neuroscience framework, and how this is a model to maintain your beautifully crafted team and flourish in happiness and contentment.

All the tools for recruitment, effective management, coaching and succession planning we uncovered can help you ensure you are bringing the best suited people into your business, and supporting them to be the best they can be, so your business can be the best it can be.

We also looked at why differentiation through customer experience is a superior differentiation strategy in terms of sustainability, and I provided my SCA framework to act as the vehicle to implement your winning customer experience strategy. This was contextualised with an example of how I rolled this out in one of my leadership roles.

Finally, we worked through certain strategic models and financial ratios to help you make the best business-level decisions to ensure your money — or that of your business — is safe, you are aligned strategically, and you're swimming in the current rather than against it.

At the end of each part, I used the case studies to analyse certain aspects outlined within the chapters of that part, and put a spotlight on how these models can work in real life across different industries and businesses. All businesses selected were thoughtfully handpicked due to their authenticity, focus and support of their people, employee value alignment to the brand, and excellence in customer experience. These businesses and brands develop customers who are raving advocates due to the people behind the brand, and who serve them — and they are successful because of it.

I hope you have enjoyed this pocket playbook, and I hope you are able take enough from it to create your own stable and high-performing workplace that gives you back some time in your day.

Thank you and good luck.

Jodi x

Keep in touch

I invite you to visit my website or Instagram to continue your learning and journey with me. Here you will find a schedule of ways we can engage to further help your own individual team or business. Contact me via the following:

- www.jodicottle.com
- @jodi.cottle

REFERENCES AND FURTHER READING

>>

Collins, J and Hansen, M (2011), *Great by Choice*, Random House Business Books.

Getz, GA and Sturdivant, FD (1989), 'The nuts and bolts of formulating differentiation strategy', *Strategy & Leadership*, 17(5), 4–9.

Hill, CWL (1988), 'Differentiation versus low cost or differentiation and low cost: A contingency framework', *Academy of Management Review*, 13(3), 401–412.

Johnson, G, Scholes, K and Whittington, R (2008), *Exploring corporate strategy: Text & cases*, Prentice Hall.

Kehoe, J (2008), *Mind Power into the 21st Century*, Zoetic.

Olson, J (2016), *The Slight Edge: Turning simple disciplines into massive success & happiness.* In House Publishing (GOKO).

Payne, AF, Storbacka, K and Frow, P (2008), 'Managing the co-creation of value', *Journal of the Academy of Marketing Science*, Vol 36, 83–96.

Ray, LS (2018), *Advanced Diploma of Neuroscience Leadership Learner Guide*, NeuroCapability.

Rock, D (2009), *Your Brain at Work: Strategies for overcoming distraction, regaining focus, and working smarter all day long*, HarperCollins.

Roberts, C and Alpert, F (2010), 'Total customer engagement: designing and aligning key strategic elements to achieve growth', *Journal of Product & Brand Management*, Vol 19(3), 198–209.

Sharp, B and Dawes, J (2010), 'What is differentiation and how does it work?', *Journal of Marketing Management*, Vol 17(7–8): 739–759.

Steffen, PR, Hedges, D and Matheson, R (2022), 'The brain is adaptive not triune: How the brain responds to threat, challenge, and change', *Frontiers in Psychiatry*, 13.

Storbacka, K and Lehtinen, J (2001), *Customer Relationship Management: Creating competitive advantage through win–win relationship strategies*. McGraw-Hill.

Tulshyan, R and Burey, J (2021), 'Stop telling women they have imposter syndrome', *Harvard Business Review*.

Watkins, MD (2013), *The First 90 Days: Proven strategies for getting up to speed faster and smarter*, Updated and Expanded Edition, Harvard Business Review Press.

Whitmore, J (2017), *Coaching for Performance: The principles and practices of coaching and leadership*, 5th Edition, John Murray.

Woollett, K and Maguire, EA (2011), 'Acquiring "the Knowledge" of London's layout drives structural brain changes', *Current Biology*, Dec 20; 21(24-2): 2109–2114.

Zomerdijk, LG and Voss, CA (2010), 'Service design for experience-centric services', *Journal of Service Research*, 13(1), 67–82.

CASE STUDY RESOURCE LIST

>>>>>>>>>>>>>>>>>>>>>>>>>>>>>>>>>>>

Janine Allis and Boost Juice

(2021), 'Janine Allis on love, fear and living a life without limits' The Suite Collective, thesuitecollective.com/janine-allis-love-fear-business-success/.

Boost Juice (2019), *Boost Study Guide*, www.boostjuice.com.au/downloads/Boost_Study_Kit.pdf.

Gibbs, S (2019), '"There were times I got it all wrong": Boost Juice founder Janine Allis reveals how she built a $350 million empire from her kitchen', *Daily Mail*, 18 August.

Lightbody, D (2019), 'In conversation: Janine Allis' leadership tips', The Leadership Institution, www.theleadership institute.com.au/2019/04/from-relationship-breakdown-to-the-wrong-people-why-business-fail/.

White, S (2019), 'Boost Juice founder, Janine Allis', *The Sydney Morning Herald*, 19 January.

Natalie Brennan and Muffin Break

(2020), 'Natalie Brennan, Food Co Group,' Shopping Centre News, www.shoppingcentrenews.com.au/shopping-centre-news/retail-outlook/natalie-brennan-food-co/.

Collins, J (2018), 'Female leader, Natalie Brennan, General Manager Muffin Break', Femeconomy, femeconomy.com/female-leader-natalie-brennan-general-manager-muffin-break/.

Z Energy

(2012), 'Z Energy wins highest praise', *Nelson Mail*, 16 June.

Hamish, M (2013), 'Z Energy celebrates as 510 staff get certificates', *Manawatu Standard*.

Hunter, T (2013), 'Smart team behind Z offer', Stuff, www.stuff.co.nz/business/money/8995604/Smart-team-behind-Z-offer.

Z Energy (2012), *Annual Review 2012*, https://znz-webbackendassets-s3bucket-prod.s3.ap-southeast-2.amazonaws.com/public/zenergy/about-z/documents/2012-Annual-Review.pdf.

Z Energy (2013), *Annual Review 2013*, https://znz-webbackendassets-s3bucket-prod.s3.ap-southeast-2.amazonaws.com/public/zenergy/about-z/documents/2013-Annual-Review.pdf.

Z Energy (2023), 'About Z', www.z.co.nz/about-z/.

Strong Pilates

Kelly, P and Reilly, D (2022), 'Michael Ramsey on building the number one F45 studio on the planet & how Strong Pilates is now taking over', *Little Fish* podcast, www.littlefishproperties.com.au/michael-ramsey-little-fish-podcast-ep-12/.

Laine, R (2022), 'STRONG Pilates is a game-changing new gym combining rowing and Pilates, Urban List, www.theurbanlist.com/sunshinecoast/a-list/strong-pilates.

Dedovic, A (2022), 'After taking Australia by storm, Rowformer fitness brand STRONG Pilates steers towards UK', Business News Australia, www.businessnewsaustralia.com/articles/going-global--studio-fitness-brand-strong-pilates-to-roll-out-three-uk-locations-next-year.html.

INDEX